POI

LIBRARY

A Surviv

ALSO BY MARK YAKICH

Poetry Collections

Unrelated Individuals Forming a Group Waiting to Cross
The Making of Collateral Beauty
The Importance of Peeling Potatoes in Ukraine
Green Zone New Orleans
Poetry for Planes
Spiritual Exercises

POETRY

A Survivor's Guide

MARK YAKICH

Bloomsbury Academic
An imprint of Bloomsbury Publishing Inc

B L O O M S B U R Y
NEW YORK • LONDON • OXFORD • NEW DELHI • SYDNEY

Bloomsbury Academic

An imprint of Bloomsbury Publishing Inc

1385 Broadway	50 Bedford Square
New York	London
NY 10018	WC1B 3DP
USA	UK

www.bloomsbury.com

BLOOMSBURY and the Diana logo are trademarks of Bloomsbury Publishing Plc

First published 2016

Library of Congress Cataloging-in-Publication Data
Yakich, Mark.
Poetry : a survivor's guide / Mark Yakich.
pages cm
Includes index.
Summary: "A provocative and practical guide, written for students of creative writing as well as literary studies, to an art form that is both loved and feared"– Provided by publisher.
ISBN 978-1-5013-0950-2 (hardback) – ISBN 978-1-5013-0950-2 (paperback) 1. Poetry. 2. Creative writing. I. Title.
PN1031.Y35 2015
808.1–dc23
2015018669

ISBN: HB: 978-1-5013-0950-2
PB: 978-1-5013-0949-6
ePub: 978-1-5013-0951-9
ePDF: 978-1-5013-0952-6

Typeset by Integra Software Services Pvt. Ltd.
Printed and bound in the United States of America

For my students

Beware of advice, even this.

—Carl Sandburg

CONTENTS

Writing

WARNING

This book is a survivor's guide. Not *the* survivor's guide—just one of many possibilities.

Maybe you've picked it up because something inside you said or is saying, *I must have poetry as I must have air!* or *I think poetry might be good for me, like a piece of fresh fruit or a handful of nuts.* Maybe there's another reason entirely. Whatever the case, please know that the propositions, tenets, and techniques that follow are merely techniques, tenets, and propositions. What some readers may find serious or imperative, others will find whimsical or impractical. What some may find useful, others won't—and vice versa. If there's a single aim here, it is to help you understand and experience language as a system of and in play. As Kafka once said, *A book must be an axe for the frozen sea inside us.* But it may be equally stimulating to recast his sentence: *A book is a frozen sea waiting for the axe inside us.*

Let us, then, break ice.

Introduction

Today I am a poet. But that may be only because for a long time I wasn't. As a child I found the little tomes of Dr. Seuss insufferable, and I enjoyed the itsy-bitsy spider not for its sweet song but for Mother's delicate fingernail tickles. I checked books out of the library because my parents and sister did: each of us would get the borrower's limit of twenty books, and back at home I'd dutifully haul them upstairs to my room and set them on my nightstand. Over the two-week lending period, I'd ignore the books except to note how well or poorly they provided decoration to the room. The night before they were due, I would pick up the tower, topple it onto the bed, and study the covers as one would the surfaces of rocks. I don't recall any of the books ever including poems, but they could have—I rarely opened them.

In grade and middle school, the only thing I remember reading and writing were love letters, carefully folded in triangles like the flags of remote countries I couldn't name. And looking back, I believe I wrote and read those letters because they seemed to be required by the romance of cartoons and sitcoms.

The first poem I remember hating was Coleridge's "Kubla Khan," on which I had to write a report in tenth grade. My English teacher's name was Mrs. Vrba (pronounced—yes—*ver-ba*). She had a broken foot for most of the year, and I had once arm-wrestled her daughter Tricia in seventh grade. Tricia and I had been at the State Science Fair at the University of Illinois at Champaign-Urbana. I took first place with a zoology project about how horseshoe magnets affected earthworms (Mother's idea; she also typed and wrote most of the report; I was proficient at the design and stenciling of the peg board; Father did the sawing and the screwing); but more importantly I took Tricia's hands in mine in the indoor/outdoor pool at the Howard Johnson's one barely lit afternoon. I hope Tricia, too, can still recall how we detained each other in that lukewarm bath, our hands glossing each other's trunks. Telling myself this story of Tricia during her mother's poetry lessons was the only way I saw poetry as relevant: it served merely as a distraction from real life.

In college I took one English class (expository writing), and I majored in political science. Instead of love letters, there was now lovemaking. I enjoyed it much more than writing, and hoped that my partners did as well. Before I was twenty-five, I had read three novels, of which two were *The Catcher in the Rye*. That's not a boast; rather, it's something I'm ashamed of—like a fear of flying. But when I was twenty-five I moved to Belgium on a research grant and began living in a one-room lean-to attached to a fourteenth-century building in the small college town of Leuven where everyone around me spoke Flemish. In other words, I was isolated and had no friends. I soon realized, however, that books and the voices in them made for decent companionship. And because most poems are brief, I could make a lot of friends fast.

For years I wouldn't admit to being a poet. The role seemed wholly unfit for modern life. Now I am a professor and teach poetry for a living, which, to me, is at once a silly and vital occupation. The poet Marianne Moore once called poetry contemptible and genuine in the same breath, which is not the same thing as calling it genuinely contemptible. For the same reason poetry is irrelevant as compared to, say, heart surgery or firefighting or trash collecting, it is also important. Because poetry doesn't make money, it almost always escapes commodification.

Poetry's irrelevance, therefore, becomes its importance. And the two qualities link up in my head, as in this poem by A. R. Ammons:

Small Song

The reeds give
way to the
wind and give
the wind away

These four lines were some of the first lines of poetry I ever enjoyed. I could and could not make out what they were telling me. These seven words (a few repeated) couldn't have been any simpler and yet they made (and still make) my mind do little backflips. As in W. B. Yeats' famous line *How can we know the dancer from the dance?* I still keep trying to discern which is which: Are the reeds only reedy because they're moved by the wind, or is the wind only windy because we detect its effects? It is, of course, not necessary to decide between the two. But no matter how many times I read the poem, I feel ridiculously compelled to pick one over the other—as if I've just survived an airplane's water landing and must choose between my wife or our son, only one of whom I can save.

*

For poetry, according to any number of young, emerging, or weathered poets, is all about survival. Not the I'm-good-in-an-emergency kind, but the let's-get-through-this-day kind. The truth is that being a survivor often simply comes down to being alive. Being your own star witness to the ending that is always inside you. And being considerate to all those who came before. The fathers and mothers who got together and sometimes loved each other; their endings, too, are in you. All those screaming nights, sleep-filled babies, beans harvested as they were dying on the vines. All those men who killed other men—religion or not—bludgeoned them with rocks, gutted them with sharpened sticks—blood for honey, flies atop dead bodies—and all those women who were taken in caves or behind bushes or on downy meadows and then lobbed over cliffs. The dead and the super dead. The thousands of generations, all of it—evolution or not—coming to a head right now. Your head, literally, so that if you put your middle finger gently into your ear, you can hear the low-pitched hum of a spacecraft travelling through time. Earth. And yet here you are, still as a book splayed on a shelf, bored by the idea of looking at the stars one more time.

No one should tell you how or what to think, I know. It feels oppressive or tedious, or it intimates that you be humbler than you are. When I was a student of creative writing programs, I too was an ironist-cum-sentimentalist. And I desperately sought a guide that would help me survive what I had gotten myself into. Help me, that is, to understand poetry without obfuscating it in literary jargon or dumbing down the practice of writing as variations of "write what you know" or breezy workouts in form. Too many texts were either dry primers bent on rote knowledge (e.g., What is a synecdoche? Who was Hamlet's best friend?), or theoretical tracts with esoteric agendas (e.g., "What is that tension between the temporal decay of voice and the expectation of lyric closure if not the formal mapping of the dynamics of desire?"). Such books, I imagine, have their respective places in poetry, but neither provides a practical *and* enjoyable guide about how poems work or how to engage them outside of the classroom.

In my own classroom, I have made my students watch a three-minute and nine second highlight video of Chicago Bears running back Walter Payton, on repeat, for entire meetings. I have made them write essays comparing and contrasting ontology and oncology using words that contain only the vowel "o." I have let them grade each other's writing based on sound effects exclusively, with no regard for meaning, context, or rules of syntax and grammar. I have written on the board, *You have just died, write the eulogy your mother or father must give*, left the room, and waited outside the building to ambush them in a skeleton costume. (Actually, my five-year-old wore the shirt and pants and collected the drafts; I merely grimaced under the mask.)

The point of such antics is to alter our expectations just enough so that we recognize our expectations. These are efforts not only to feel more alive, but to re-experience how strange being alive at any particular moment really is. As the poet Paul Celan remarks, "Reality is not simply there, it does not simply exist: it must be sought out and won."

Or it doesn't. Living and dying follow no step-by-step guide; as well, reading or writing a poem follows no set method. Of course you can follow this book page-by-page from beginning to end, but it's probably as valuable to open it anywhere and cut your own path. There's no grand narrative here, as in a story or novel. Instead, do as you would with a collection of poems. Begin where chance takes you.

Let me take, for instance, a new book that arrived in the mail this morning. I sit down with it at my desk and soon realize that it's both a collection and a writing guide. At random I open to an exercise that asks me to sit on the floor, affix a helium-filled, red balloon to my navel with a piece of chewing gum, clip and tape some of my hair to the balloon, close my eyes, lick the balloon, let go of the balloon, lie down, conjure up the image of my mother birthing me, and then start writing. What a bizarre and daring prompt! But the example poem that follows, written by the author from the exercise, is a dud. This guide may be no different: you are as apt to find something that you like as you are to find something that you don't like. No worries. This book has no LIKE button. In fact, my hope is not even that your likes will outnumber your dislikes. My hope is that these pages will reanimate your thinking about what a poem is and what a poem can be.

*

When I used to ask students what a poem is, I would get answers like "a painting in words," or "a medium for self-expression," or "a song that rhymes and displays beauty." None of these answers ever really satisfied me, or them, and so for a while I stopped asking the question.

Then one time, I requested that my students bring in to class something that had a personal meaning to them. With their objects on their desks, I gave them three prompts: first, to write a paragraph about why they brought in the item; second, to write a paragraph describing the item empirically, as a scientist might; and third, to write a paragraph in the first-person from the point of view of the item. The first two were warm-ups, red herrings. Above the third paragraph I told them to write "Poem."

Here is what one student wrote:

Poem

I might look weird or terrifying, but really I'm a device that helps people breathe. Under normal circumstances nobody needs me. I mean, I'm only used for emergencies and even then only for a limited time. If you're lucky, you'll never have to use me. Then again, I can see some future time when everybody will have to carry me around.

The item he had brought to class? A gas mask. The point of this exercise wasn't only to illustrate the malleability of language or the playfulness of writing, but to present the idea that a poem is a strange thing which operates as nothing else in the world does.

I suppose most of us have known poems are strange ever since we were infants being put to bed with lullabies like "Rock-a-bye baby," or were children being taught prayers that begin "Our Father who art in Heaven … ." The questions soon arose: What idiot put that cradle in a tree? And what's art got to do with my Daddy-God? But this kind of strangeness we got used to. And later, at some point in school, we asked or were made to ask again: What is a poem?

For example, in high school my English teacher handed me Matthew Arnold's "Dover Beach" and said I had to write an essay about what it meant. I couldn't make heads or tails out of the assignment, and the poem became the object of my hatred. The poem seemed willfully *not* to make sense. I soon found every poem to be an irritation, a blotch of words, a ludicrous puzzle that got in the way of true understanding as well as true feeling.

Unless you are a poet or writer, it's likely that poems have apprehended you less and less as the years have passed. Occasionally, in a magazine or online you see one—with its ragged right edge and arbitrary-looking line breaks—and it announces itself by what it is not: prose that runs continuously from the left to the right margins of the page. A poem practically dares you not just to look but to read: *I am different. I am special. I am other. Ignore me at your peril.*

And so you read it and too often become disappointed by its blandness, how it can be paraphrased with an easy moral, such as "this too shall pass" or "getting old sucks"—how essentially it's no different in content than most of the prose around it. Or, you become disappointed because the poem baffles initial comprehension. It's inaccessible in its fragmented syntax and grammar, or obscure in its allusions. Nevertheless, you pat yourself on the back for trying.

How many of us believe poetry is useless? How many of us don't even care to ask the question, Is poetry useless?

Comparatively, a poem moves a reader, physically or emotionally, very rarely. Other media are much better at bringing us to tears—television, the movies. And if we want the news, we read an article online or glean our Twitter feed. If we want something between tears and the news, we just stare at our children when they ask a question that sounds more like a statement: "Why do grown-ups drink so much beer?"

But seriously, isn't a poem a home for deep feelings, dazzling imagery, arresting lyricism, tender reflections, and/or biting wit? I suppose so. But, again, other arts or technologies seem better at those jobs—novels offer us real or imaginary worlds to explore or escape to, tweets offer us poignant epigrams, painting and design offer us eye candy, and music—well, face it, poetry has never been able to compete with that sublime combo of lyrics, instruments, and melody.

There is at least one kind of utility that a poem can embody: ambiguity. Ambiguity is not what school or society wants to instill. You don't want an ambiguous answer as to which side of the road you should drive on, or whether or not pilots should put down the flaps before takeoff. That said, day-to-day living—unlike sentence-to-sentence reading—is filled with ambiguity: *Does she love me enough to marry? Should I fuck him one more time before I dump him?*

But such observations still don't tell us much about what a poem really is. Try crowdsourcing for an answer. If you search Wikipedia for "poem," it redirects to "poetry": "a form of literary art which uses aesthetic and rhythmic qualities of language—such as phonoaesthetics, sound symbolism, etc." Fine English-professor speak, but it belies the origins of the word. "Poem" comes from the Greek *poíēma*, meaning a "thing made," and a poet is defined in ancient terms as "a maker of things." So if a poem is a thing made, what kind of thing is it?

I've heard other poets define poems in organic terms: wild animals—natural, untamable, unpredictable, raw. But the metaphor quickly falls apart. Such animals live on their own, utterly unconcerned with the names humans put upon them. In inorganic terms, the poet William Carlos Williams called poems "little machines," as he treated them as mechanical, human-engineered, and precise. But here too, the metaphor breaks down. A worn-out part on an automobile can be switched out with a nearly identical part and run as it did before. In a poem, a word exchanged for another word (even a close synonym) can alter the entire functioning of the poem.

The most productive thing about trying to define a poem through comparison—to an animal, a machine, or whatever else—is not in the comparison itself but in the arguing over it. Whether or not you view a poem as a machine or a wild animal, it can change the machine or wild animal of your mind. A poem helps the mind play with its well-trod patterns of thought, and can even help reroute those patterns by making us see the familiar anew.

An example: the sun. It can be dictionary-defined as "that luminous celestial body around which the earth and other planets revolve." But it can also be described as a four-year-old intuits while staring out the car window on a long winter's drive: "Mom, isn't the sun just a kind of space-heater?" Another example: honey. According to the dictionary, it's "a sweet, sticky yellowish-brown fluid made by bees from the nectar they collect from flowers." According to mothers everywhere, it's "bee spit that can kill an infant."

The poem as mental object is no difficult reach, especially if we consider the extent to which pop song lyrics can literally get stuck, as the neuroscientists tell us, in the form of "earworms" in the synapses of the brain. The intermingling of words and melody has an historied potency going back to schoolyard rhymes that call attention to metalanguage: "Sticks and stones may break my bones, but words can never hurt me." That line itself can hurt, paradoxically, as it perhaps invokes the memory of being called hideous names, whether personalized (Yakich jock-itch) or generalized (camel-jockey).

But when are words most like sticks and stones?

Consider a poem lurking in the pages of *The New Yorker*. There it is staring you in the face: Do you read it as well as it reads you? In terms of ink on paper, it does nothing more than the prose around it, but in terms of apprehension, it draws in your eye and places the poem in a rarefied position and a totally ignorable one all at once. *Oh, look, it's a precious little chit of words! What a waste of my time!*

But there's also all that white space surrounding it. How much did that cost? The magazine gave up valuable space to print the poem instead of printing a longer article or an advertisement. Nobody bought the copy of *The New Yorker* for the poem, except perhaps for the poet who wrote it. A poem is a text—a product of writing and rewriting—but unlike articles, stories, or novels, it never really becomes a thing made in order to become a commodity.

A new novel, a memoir, or even a short story collection has the potential for earning big bucks. Of course, this potential is often not realized, but a new book of poems that yields its author more than a thousand-dollar advance is exceedingly rare. Publicists at publishing houses, even the largest ones, dutifully write press releases and send out review copies of poetry collections, but none will tell you that they expect a collection to sell enough copies to break even with the costs of printing it. Like no other book, a book of poems presents itself not as a thing for the marketplace, but as a thing for its own sake.

The epitome of such "sake-ness" are poems that put their "made-ness" right in your face. Variously called visual poems, concrete poems, shape poems, or calligrammes, George Herbert's "Easter Wings" is a canonical example from the seventeenth century:

Lord, who createdst man in wealth and store,
Though foolishly he lost the same,
Decaying more and more,
Till he became
Most poore:
With thee
O let me rise
As larks, harmoniously,
And sing this day thy victories:
Then shall the fall further the flight in me.

My tender age in sorrow did beginne
And still with sicknesses and shame
Thou didst so punish sinne,
That I became
Most thinne.
With thee
Let me combine,
And feel this day thy victorie:
For, if I imp my wing on thine,
Affliction shall advance the flight in me.

The poem's wings, of birds or angels, coincide or illustrate the textual content: the speaker's desire to reach skyward toward the Lord. The visual form provides what we might call a little bonus or lagniappe in meaning, and it also makes us notice the poem as more than a raggedly blotch—the blotch itself is meaning.

In the nineteenth century, the French poet Stéphane Mallarmé pushed this page-as-canvas idea even further in *Un coup de dés jamais n'abolira le hasard* ("A Throw of the Dice Will Never Abolish Chance"). Published in a variety of editions over the past hundred years, his book-length poem not only manipulates black type, font styles, and white space, but also it exploits the boundaries of the page itself, including the gutter—the seam in the middle of a book—which serves as the alley in which the "dice" (i.e., words) are thrown.

Because the poem allows the reader to make multiple connections between phrases and lines—reading across, down, in combination, or according to specific fonts—some scholars view *Un coup de dés* as a precursor to hypertext. As a reader, you have a certain amount of "freedom" in navigating the poem. The caveat is that freedom often requires more work, more self-motivation, and a certain degree of confusion.

Which brings us back to poetry's contemporary predicament: a poem that is so strange, so other, is also a poem many feel they might as well ignore. Here's a poem from the 1960s by Aram Saroyan:

lighght

Yes, that's the whole poem. I know, it seems asinine. When I wrote it on the board and asked my students to examine it, one said, "How do you even read it aloud?" When we tried, we began to understand the intent of the poem. The word "light" seems to be implied, but what's with the apparent typo? After a long silence, another student said, "That's the point—in the ordinary word 'light' we don't pronounce the 'gh'—the 'gh' is silent, and the double 'gh' makes us realize that even more." The poem calls attention to the system of language itself—the stuff of letters in combination—and the relationship between sound and sense. The familiar—a plain word such as "light"—has been made new if only for a brief moment. In Saroyan's own words, "[T]he crux of the poem is to try and make the ineffable, which is light—which we only know about because it illuminates something else—into a *thing*."

When we come across a poem—any poem—our first assumption should not be to prejudice it as a thing of beauty, but simply as a thing. The linguists and theorists tell us that language is all metaphor in the first place. The word "apple" has no inherent link with that bright red, edible object on my desk right now. But the intricacies of signifiers and signifieds fade from view after college. Because of its special status—set apart in a magazine or a book, all that white space pressing upon it—a poem still has the ability to surprise, if only for a moment which is outside all the real and virtual, the aural and digital chatter that envelopes it, and us.

One might argue that the page is just a metaphor for all that can't be put on it, and that a poem is merely a substitution, for better or for worse, for a lived feeling or event. And yet, one Jewish tradition admonishes that parents teach their children to love the Talmud not by reading it to them first, but by having them lick honey from its pages. That would seem, to me, an ideal way to experience both bee spit and poetry.

Reading

At one time or another, when face-to-face with a poem, most everyone has been perplexed. The experience of reading a poem itself is as likely to turn us off, intellectually or emotionally, as it is to move us. Unless patronized by celebrities, set to music, accompanied by visuals, or penned by our own children, poems do a terrible job of marketing themselves. All those ragged lines and affected white spaces make them appear as though they should be treated only as pieces of solemn art. *Look but don't get too close, and definitely don't touch.*

But what if the fine art of reading poetry isn't so fine after all? What if the predicament about poems is precisely our well-intentioned but ill-fitting dispositions toward reading them?

Essentials

Dispel the notion that reading poetry is going to dramatically change your life. Your life is continually changing; most of the time you're simply too busy to pay enough attention to it. Poems ask you to pay attention—that's all.

When you read a poem, especially a poem *not* meant to be a "spoken word" poem, always read it out loud. (Never mind what they said in grammar school—to subvocalize so that you won't bother your peers.) Your ear will pick up more than your head will allow. That is, the ear will tell the mind what to think.

There are two ways to read a poem out loud: by minding the line breaks, adding brief pauses at the end of each line; or, by following the punctuation, whether or not it matches up with the end of the line. Neither way is better than the other in any essential way. But reading as though the line break is punctuation (a pause) will sound more affected (possibly pretentious) than reading as though the lines are all prose. As a matter of examination or composition, read by overemphasizing the end-of-the-line pause. As a matter of performance (as at a poetry reading), read to the punctuation.

Try to meet a poem on its terms not yours. If you have to "relate" to a poem in order to understand it, you aren't reading it sufficiently. In other words, don't try to fit the poem into your life.

Try to see what world the poem creates. Then, if you are lucky, its world will help you re-see your own.

Marianne Moore said that poems are "imaginary gardens with real toads in them." Translation: (a) a poem gives you a sense of the world but in a world of its own sense; and (b) all life is an imaginary garden, and we are the toads.

Is a poem real or artificial? One answer: a poem is all real while you are reading it and it is all artificial because it was written down for you to read.

Whether or not you are conscious of it, you are always looking for an excuse to stop reading a poem and move on to another poem or to do something else entirely. Resist this urge as much as possible. Think of it as a Buddhist regards a pesky gnat. The gnat, like the poem, may be irritating, but it's not going to kill you to brave it for a little while longer.

"Reading for pleasure" implies there's "reading for displeasure" or "reading for pain." All reading should be pleasurable: Like sex, it pleases to a greater or lesser degree, but pleasure ultimately isn't the only point.

When you come across something that appears "ironic," make sure it's not simply the speaker's sarcasm or your own disbelief.

Reading a poem will probably at first create a picture in your mind. A set of objects, a character, a scene. But it need not do this. Sometimes a poem will create a frame for a picture or the outline of a puzzle but not provide a single piece. Sometimes all you get is the piece—what some call a lyric.

Perform marginalia. Reading without writing in the margins is like walking without moving your arms. You can do it and still reach your destination, but it'll always feel like you're missing something essential about the activity.

The idea that a poem can be interpreted in an infinite number of ways is patently false. There may be a handful of ways, but that doesn't mean that examining a poem is a free-for-all. Reading poems is a practice. And it helps to practice reading all kinds of poems, especially those you've never seen before—new or old.

The very best way to read a poem is perhaps to be young, intelligent, and slightly drunk. There is no doubt, however, that reading poems in old age cultivates a desire to have read more poems in youth.

The trick to reading poetry is to find poems you like! It can be hard going. You can take the simple step of subscribing to one of the free "poem-a-day" services offered by the Poetry Foundation,

Academy of American Poets, etc. They'll send you a poem (variously new and old) each morning. Some will be to your liking, some won't. Just don't worry about those that don't stay with you, and keep going. Or, you can take a larger leap and seek out the poetry section of a university library. At random pick a book off the shelf, thumb its pages. When you find poems you like, put the book in a stack until you have about ten books. This may take you an hour or a few hours. Check out the books, take them home, and put them on the kitchen table. Pore over them at meals instead of poring over a screen. Make it a practice: checking out books and returning them on their due dates. Do this for a year and you'll be better read in poetry than the vast majority of English PhDs.

There is nothing really lost in reading a poem. If you don't understand the poem, you lose little time or energy. On the contrary, there is potentially much to gain—a new thought, an old thought seen anew, or simply a moment separated from all the other highly structured moments of your time.

Someday, when all your material possessions will seem to have shed their utility and just become obstacles to the toilet, poems will still hold their value. They are rooms that take up such little room. A memorized poem, or a line or two, becomes part internal jewelry and part life-saving skill, like knowing how to put a mugger in an arm-lock or the best way to cut open a mango without slicing your hand.

We don't remember poems; we remember aphoristic lines from poems. Or we misremember them and are still pleased.

Poetic Aims

Horace was right when he said that poetry should "inform and delight." Though not all poems do both. And some do neither.

Some poems teach a moral or spin a yarn. Others reflect, ruminate, or meditate.

Some prophesize or warn. Others offer catharsis, shock, or gibberish. Some lament and protest. Others document or memorialize. Still others transform the page or screen into a canvas for mark-making, or into a map for syntactic exploration.

Poems can do many of these things at the same time. Be aware, however, that other arts and disciplines may be better suited to accomplish these aims. Novels have their complex narratives. Movies: their combinations of picture, sound, and story. Videogames: their mesmerization. Plastic arts: their displays of creators' hands. Photographs: their frozen moments of time. Philosophy: its speculation. Neuropsychology: its probing of cognition and behavior. Social work: its social justice. And dance: its sublime destruction of the knees.

Emily Dickinson articulated the purpose of poetry like this: "Tell all the truth but tell it slant." Why slant? So that we can re-see what we so often take for granted. In a good poem something familiar is made unfamiliar, perhaps even strange. Freud called this phenomenon *Das Unheimliche* ("the uncanny"). The critic Viktor Shklovsky termed it *ostranenie* ("defamiliarization"). And T. S. Eliot, in one of his *Four Quartets*, put the entire project of poems (and life) like this: "We shall not cease from exploration/And the end of all our exploring/Will be to arrive where we started/And know the place for the first time."

Accessibility

People will tell you there are two kinds of poems: the "accessible" poem whose intent and meaning are easy to appreciate, and the "inaccessible" or "obscure" poem whose intent and meaning are difficult to appreciate. It's up to you how hard you want to work.

If you don't know a word, look it up or die.

A poem cannot be paraphrased. In fact, a poem's greatest potential lies in the opposite of paraphrase: ambiguity. Ambiguity is at the center of what is it to be a human being. We really have no idea what's going to happen from moment to moment, but we have to act as if we do.

Difficult poems often intend to be so. What was previously a pattern-making of ambiguity gets pushed to sheer arbitrariness. This may mean that there is no "higher" meaning than in the moment of the experience of reading the poem. There is nothing to look to, nothing to explicate, nothing to do but read it again and again, inhabiting the reading and the moment as fully as possible. What Stein once called "the continuous present."

Mystery is more important than clarity in poetry. Or rather clarity is important but only when one doesn't at first recognize it as clarity. Dickinson more than Whitman embodies this. Her poems give us a clarity we didn't know before. Whitman's simply show us everything and dare us to look.

A poem has no hidden meaning, only "meanings" you've not yet realized are right in front of you. Discerning subtleties takes practice. Reading poetry is a convention like anything else. And you learn the rules of it like anything else—e.g., driving a car, baking a cake, walking a tightrope.

To assist you in reading contemporary poems that use associative logic as a guiding principle, begin with Lawrence Sterne's novel *The Life and Opinions of Tristram Shandy, Gentleman*. To help with juxtaposition, examine the sentence-to-sentence linkages in the "Findings" sections of *Harper's Magazine* and in Joe Brainard's *I Remember*. Then, try the more difficult work of poets such as John Ashbery, Lyn Hejinian, Michael Palmer, Elizabeth Willis, or Ann Lauterbach.

One of the best ways to read an "inaccessible" poem is by examining the interaction of its various "idioms." Not idiomatic phrases, per se, but idioms as Mikhail Bakhtin suggests in his concept of heteroglossia. Don't be put off by the invented term, which he employed to study novels. Heteroglossia involves identifying different types of speech or language or registers in a text. Possibilities include dense imagery, literary tropes, scientific language, purple prose, abstract language, philosophical discourse, dialogue, clichés, vernacular, and slang. In any poem, you can identify the various idioms at work, noting possible patterns and variations. In a difficult poem, these idioms may get incredibly dense, often brushing and butting up against each other, line by line or even phrase by phrase, causing ambiguity or incomprehension at exactly the spot in the poem that warrants the closest discernment.

To comprehend a difficult text is to question it relentlessly. This can't be done in the mind alone. If you're not scrawling all over it with arrows, questions, squiggles, etc., you're getting little, if anything, out of your reading.

A poem can feel like a locked safe in which the combination is hidden inside. In other words, it's okay if you don't understand a poem. Sometimes it takes dozens of readings to come to the slightest understanding. And sometimes understanding never comes. It's the same with being alive: wonder and confusion mostly prevail.

Emerson talked about being in one's time as being "on a stair"— all the other stairs, other moments in time, past and future, below or ahead of you. You can only read from your stair, and so reading poems from the very past past may feel difficult … but relax. Take a breath. That seemingly impenetrable poem is perhaps not about pinning down meaning; it's about pinning you down. To make you, at least for a moment, sit still.

A poem isn't a Rorschach blot. Or it's a Rorschach blot in the guise of a poet's shadow.

Try reading that unusual poem—always out loud—as fast as you can, noting where you stumble the most. Then try reading it abnormally slow, as if you have an aphasia—three or more seconds between each word. Your eyes will want to run ahead and then back and then ahead again—let them. But keep the silences between reading aloud each word. Between your speed reading and your super slow reading an unfamiliar understanding can develop, one in which the poem can begin to puncture your usual way of understanding.

If a poem is particularly hard to read, try reading it as one might a painting—let your eye fall anywhere. Begin in the middle, at a random word, read a phrase as slowly as you can, aloud, staring at each word for three or four seconds. Or, scan the poem's shape, looking at lines as if brushstrokes. Or, begin reading from the last line and move upwards to see if it makes more sense. The idea is to find an initial entry point, and then later, eventually, you may discover the beginning.

Biography

As hard as it sounds, separate the poet from the speaker of the poem. A poet always wears a mask (persona) even if she isn't trying to wear a mask, and so to equate poet and speaker denies the poem any imaginative force that lies outside of her lived life.

Although it is supremely difficult to approach Sylvia Plath's work without wanting to reach in and pull her head back from the oven, learn from her singular, masterful use of figurative language. From her posthumous *Ariel*: "Love set you going like a fat gold watch." "I am nude as a chicken neck, does nobody love me?" "Your body/Hurts me as the world hurts God. I am a lantern—" "I see your cute décor/Close on you like the fist of a baby/Or an anemone, that sea/Sweetheart, that kleptomaniac."

If you still have trouble keeping Plath out of the kitchen, consider that she wasn't all doom and gloom. Witness: Ted Hughes' version of *Ariel* ends with the lines "From the bottom of the pool, fixed stars/Govern a life."; but Plath's version, the one she ordered in manuscript before she died, ends like this: "The bees are flying. They taste like spring."

Reading is a perversion. A reader will, inevitably, want to come to know a particular author so thoroughly that he will want to embrace him, kiss him, even stroke his long beard. But an author only wants to touch a reader with his words; otherwise, he would have done something different with his life, such as become a podiatrist or a hairdresser.

The lesson that we are taught as children not to write in books— that they are sacred and thus should be cared for gently—is erroneous. Sacred objects don't have to be treated as barely touchable ones. By writing, or drawing, in a book, one doesn't disrespect the text or its author. On the contrary, writing in a book is the ultimate homage. Let us not think that books are so precious that we can't put our own "stamps" or "signatures" into them—that we can't mingle our biographies with theirs.

The biography of a poet matters most to other poets, either as a source of motivation out of envy to write better poems, or as a way of quid-pro-quo community-making. When poets care about each other more as individuals more than they care for those individuals' poems, a community is born.

Be suspect of all well-held notions of biography. People will tell you that Shakespeare had little regard for his wife, Anne Hathaway. Their evidence: that upon his death he bequeathed her only his "second-best" bed. What they've forgotten to say is that the "first-best" bed was reserved for guests. The second-best bed was the conjugal bed.

Hal Hartley's *Henry Fool* is the biopic of an itinerate poet who falls in love with Parker Posey. Let it be a cautionary tale about attempting the Great American Poem.

If you are of two minds about whether or not you should consult the biography of a poet when reading her poem, consider this: When a chunk of extra-sharp cheddar cheese must be thrown away because it's fallen on the dirt floor of your straw hut, are you meant to feel sad for the cow?

Poets depend on readers for confirmation of their worth. Readers depend on poets for confirmation of their doubts.

Close Reading

Students often complain that by studying a poem ("picking it apart") you take all the fun out of it. They have not yet understood that unless you have written the poem yourself, studying the poem is the only fun to be had.

It may very well be that your teacher is trying to get you to "dissect" the poem; autopsy means "see for yourself."

Close reading stems from a single question: *Why this word here?* *This* meaning diction (word choice) and *here* meaning syntax (word order). Not "why" did the poet select one particular word instead of another word (that's a question of authorial intent), but what's the *effect or expectation* of one particular word as compared to another word. For example, you're on a plane flying to Honolulu ... which would you rather hear the pilot say over the intercom: *We're going to experience some turbulence en route*, or *We're going to experience a few bumps en route*? The two sentences appear to mean the same thing, and yet they don't. *Turbulence*, a Latinate word, may sound more eloquent to some ears, as compared to *a few bumps*, an Anglo-Saxon formulation, that may sound more tangible to others. One person, that is, may say that *turbulence* sounds "nicer" than *bumps*: *Who wants to hit a bump? That sounds like it could do a lot of damage.* But another may disagree: *Turbulence is so vague ... how long will it last, an hour? I could tolerate a few bumps.* There is not a right or wrong answer here, but there is an effect or expectation that originates in asking the simple question, *Why this word here?*

If you can ask *Why this word here?* then you can also extrapolate the question, *Why this line here? Why this stanza here? Why this poem here?*

In a Station of the Metro

The apparition of these faces in the crowd;
Petals on a wet, black bough.

Ezra Pound's poem has been taught in innumerable classrooms as an illustration of the primacy of imagery. But what did we learn—that pictures are important, that the Metro is an ominous place? Let's close-read those three lines (the title functions much like a first line) by asking *Why this word here?* Why, for example, "apparition"? Let's substitute "ghost." What's the new effect? The connotations of a ghost include an ex-body, a lost soul, the color white—perhaps the ubiquitous sheet that portrays a ghost at Halloween. One might also point out that that monosyllabic Germanic "ghost" is more down to earth, less literary, and that a ghost is a continual roamer, as compared to the multisyllabic Latinate "apparition" that, to some minds, denotes a phenomenon that appears suddenly and then goes away.

One could question, too, why the line begins with "The apparition" and not simply "these faces"? Or why not try changing the order of the lines, putting "Petals on a wet, black bough" first? Like any analysis or "critical thinking," close reading involves a series of questions … and sometimes experiments. For instance, let us engage the poem by setting it beside a similar text, such as the following by Jules Renard, of about the same time (1910):

Walk in the Bois

The old women buried in the depths of carriages.
The fine swans, clothed in their snow.

Is this poem not equally imagistic and metaphorically thought-provoking? But let us replace Pound's title with Renard's.

Walk in the Bois

The apparition of these faces in the crowd;
Petals on a wet, black bough.

Switching out titles is admittedly an arbitrary act, but look at what it reveals: "Walk in the Bois" (*bois*, French for forest) quickly patterns up with the petals and bough. Looking back at Pound's original, we see now just as quickly what that poem intends: not simply to call forth imagery, but to mix city and nature specifically, to put forth an urban pastoral.

To get at poems is a matter of honing your close reading skills as well as sharpening your sense of play.

There may be no better way of close reading a poem than memorizing it. In the process you will get hung up on certain words, line breaks, odd-to-you phrasings—exactly the kind of work close reading entails. But sitting in a room learning a poem by heart can be extraordinarily boring. Venture out, then, hand in hand with your poem (hard copy, not digital) and roam city streets when it's still dark in early morning or at night. Glance down every time you reach a streetlight to take in another line, rehearsing it before you get to the next streetlight and the next line, all the way uptown, downtown, back and forth, for however long it takes to be able to fluidly recite the poem to any stranger you may bump into.

Close reading a poem helps you work up the ladder—close reading a story, an essay, a novel, etc. You ask the same kinds of questions. What can you tell, for example, from a story that begins *Young Alexander was planing wood in the kitchen*, and ends with *"Grandpa! Grandpa! They've brought your coffin."*? What's the point of the pages-long paragraphs in the novel *Blindness* by

José Saramago? In *The Great Gatsby*, a 182-page novel, the title character doesn't show up in an actual scene until p. 47; what gives? What's the effect when Toni Morrison's *The Bluest Eye* begins with the same Dick-and-Jane paragraph repeated three times, each with a slight variation? And what happens when close reading itself pulls you out of the text, into the historical context of when it was written?

Emotion

Occasionally you may feel touched by a poem—literally, as if someone has embraced you spontaneously and without cause. But this is not the case: it is you that have touched yourself.

Tolstoy argued that art's mission is to transmit emotion from one person (the creator) to another (the reader/viewer) over time and distance: "to mingle consciousness." But sometimes consciousness mingled feels a little claustrophobic...when all one wants from another person is reassurance, maybe even that indecorous but comforting lie: "Don't worry, it's all going to be okay."

There is a great deal of emotional resonance in the thought of Charlie Brown's Christmas tree—perhaps more than there is in most poems. This is nothing to lament.

So much talk about Head vs. Heart, the Emotional vs. the Intellectual ... is it not a false setup? Neuroscientists need not convince you that mind and body are inseparable or essentially the same thing: all body, all the time. Just try to have an emotion (a feeling) without first having a thought to go along with it. Emotion is thinking, a deeply mindful business. When someone says *That poem is so emotional*, he is speaking to its drama, even melodrama. When someone says *That poem is so cerebral*, she is speaking to something else—its wordplay, ambiguity, abstractions, conceptions, etc., for which a feeling exists, just not one necessarily associated with an immediate pathos/bathos.

Feelings stem from the brain, but the brain has no feeling: if your brain itself were pierced by a scalpel, you wouldn't feel a thing. Only the membrane surrounding the brain has feeling. Is this analogous to a poem's content and structure? Brain is content, membrane is structure? Or is brain the structure (non-feeling) and membrane the content (feeling)?

You come to a poem wanting to feel more than you feel, or wanting to feel what you already feel as if you've never felt it before. If your expectations are not met, you think that the poem is to blame. But the poem can never get hurt. The problem is your feelings.

Reading a good poem doesn't give you something to talk about. It silences you. Reading a great poem pushes further. It prepares you for the silence that perplexes us all: death.

Pattern and Variation

Pattern recognition. It's how our ancestors read the stars, how we domesticated animals and cultivated crops, how computers analyze and search. It's the basis of language. Whether or not you agree with Pound that literature is "charged with meaning to the utmost degree," a poem is set-piece of language, a pattern that can be experienced both as a whole and re-experienced when taken apart.

Poetry depends on pattern and variation—even non-linear, non-narrative, anti-poetic poetry. By perceiving patterns and variations on those patterns, your brain will attempt to make order out of apparent chaos. "Glockenspiel," "tadpole," and "justice" have ostensibly nothing to do with each other, and yet your brain immediately tries to piece them together simply because they are there for the apprehending.

To experience a poem is to experience its patterns. Begin with the part of a poem that first strikes you and try to *connect* it to other parts, discerning possible relationships: repetitions, echoes, congruencies, inversions, complements, etc.

A poem can have numerous patterns: of word choice, of rhythm, of sound, of imagery, of idea, of tone, of line or stanza length, of tense, of point of view, of character, etc. The patterns can feel overwhelming, so make a list or cheat-sheet for each aspect and examine one at a time, beginning with the one that seems most salient to you.

You follow a poem by following how it changes or transforms. In each aspect, therefore, discern what precisely changes or transforms. Take imagery, for example. Do the images seem small at first and grow larger, as if zooming in? Or the reverse, does the "camera" zoom out? Does an initial image get replaced or superimposed by the next one? Are the images all of a kind? Where and when do the images end, and why specifically there? If you extract all the images from the poem, what relationships can you detect?

"Poetic structure is, simply, the pattern of a poem's turning," Michael Theune writes in *Structure & Surprise*. Turning: the point of change, the point of variation. Look for specific "turning" words: and, but, yet, although, while, as, because, then, however, moreover, etc. When you begin to notice turns in poems, you begin to notice turns in the whole array of everyday texts or speech acts—formal arguments, headlines, proposals, emails, tweets, grocery lists, etc.

As your ability to read poems improves, so will your ability to read the news, novels, legal briefs, advertisements, etc. A Starbucks poster a few years ago read: *Friends are like snowflakes ... each one is unique.* How true. But isn't snow also cold and ephemeral? Let's hope our friends are not.

Reading poetry is not only about language skills. Its alleged hermetic stylizations of syntax and diction can enhance your awareness of the world, even those things that don't deal directly in words. A dress, a room, a neighborhood—all involve systems of pattern recognition and extrapolation.

Ineffability

You may justifiably be suspect of analogies, parallels, metaphors, etc., as corrupting rational thought. But figurative language is essential to orderly thinking. Even your name is metaphoric—those letters, taken together, stand in or stand for who you think you are or think you are supposed to be.

Plato famously kicked the poets out of his republic because he thought they misrepresented reality. If reality was already a kind of copy of an "ideal"—he reasoned—then a poem was a copy of a copy. A poem, in other words, was a lie. There was nothing kind about it. For Plato, poetry obscured.

Aristotle argued the reverse: that precisely the way to know the truth is through those alleged lies, which help us pull back the curtain of this reality. For Aristotle, poetry illuminated.

The paradox of Plato is that he didn't want to be called a poet but he spoke like one. And his greatest invention was Socrates who was forever trying to express what was inexpressible. Paradoxically, we have a word for this: ineffability. Things that can't be expressed satisfactorily in words: the experience of birth, the experience of death, what consciousness is, what love is, etc.

I love you. You say it and mean it and think it is good. *I love you, too.* Someone says it and means it but it's not quite the same. It suddenly feels effable.

Ineffability: all the things that touch us on the inside but can't be touched from the outside. If you want to be moved by a poem, therefore, sometimes you must pick your nose while reading it.

Getting too serious about poetry can ruin poetry. Ruin its ineffability. To begin the endeavor, you have to take seriously what others make fun of, and make fun of what others take seriously. Remember that as a child you mostly pretended to be one.

Sound Work

Someone once sang a song only for you—and you didn't understand a word of it. It was an unspeakable moment. No doubt you were a baby, no doubt it rhymed. Rhyme is most likely the first linguistic or "literary" effect you ever experienced.

As you keep reading poems, you begin to understand that the interesting thing about rhyme is less its sound effects than what the sound effects point to—the contents of the two rhyming words. Rhyming "blue" with "you" loses its coolness factor after hearing it umpteen times. But rhyming "blue" with "undo" or "stew" or "Peru" demands more attention: your brain tries to figure out what the relationship is between the two words' *contents*.

Many of the most intriguing rhymes will be those whose contents are at odds: when there is tension between the sound and the content of the words. The more tension, the more memorable the rhyme.

Attractive rhymes are those whose contents create an unusual relationship: one word categorizing the other, one word expanding on the other, one word complementing the other, one word ghosting the other, etc. For example, what do you make of these rhymes from Michael Robbins' "On Making Mixes for Girls Who Won't Give Death Metal a Chance"?

> In olden days a glimpse of stocking
> Would give me a lobotomy.
> The very thought of me!
> Out of the car, long hair, endlessly rocking.

How is "glimpse of stocking" related to "endlessly rocking"? How is "lobotomy" related to "thought of me"?

Or consider the last two stanzas of Harryette Mullen's "[go on sister sing your song]":

> members don't get weary
> add some practice to your theory
> she wants to know is it a men thing
> or a him thing

wishing him luck
she gave him lemons to suck
told him please dear
improve your embouchure

Pull out the end-line rhymes, and you have the poem's intent nut-shelled: weary/theory/ thing/thing/luck/suck/dear/embouchure.

If you want to write in rhyme, remember that end-line full rhymes are only one kind. Enjoy and pursue other possibilities:

- For slant or "near" rhyme, Dickinson is your dominatrix: ear/fair, life/shelf, own/worn, minute/astute, realm/tomb, annulled/world, supreme/home.

- For internal or "buried" rhyme, consult Poe's "The Raven," or better yet *The Best of It: New and Selected Poems* by Kay Ryan.

- For variable line-length rhyme, examine Auden's finery in "Musée des Beaux Arts," and mind the enjambment.

- For multisyllabic rhyme, witness its comic effects in Byron's *Don Juan* ("intellectual/hen-peck'd you all"), throughout Ogden Nash's poetry ("the subway jerks/a hangnail irks"), or in the lyrics from any number of musicians. Lauryn Hill: "juice under Polaris/tango in Paris"; Edward Sharpe: "pumpkin pie/Jesus Christ." But don't think it's not without its tragedy, too. Mos Def: "AIDS patients/PlayStation."

Rhyme isn't your only sonic tool. Alliteration tantalizes and rankles the mind just as well. Try echoing vowel sounds (assonance) or consonant sounds (consonance); both please the ear and often more subtly than full-on rhyme. For example, combinations of b's and p's (labial plosives) or d's and t's (dental plosives) aren't as salient as rhyme but are sure to thrill. Witness the entirety of John Donne's *Holy Sonnet* ("Batter my heart, three person'd God"), or a few lines from D. H. Tracy's "Janet's Cottage": "Over a far down a transport drops/eight paratroops for practice, as if/a girl had plucked a dandelion gone to seed."

For its use of patterned sound effects—without using end-line rhyme and without a specific rhyme scheme—examine Macbeth's "tomorrow" speech. Read it aloud, and don't worry about what it "means."

She should have died hereafter.
There would have been a time for such a word.
Tomorrow, and tomorrow, and tomorrow

Creeps in this petty pace from day to day
To the last syllable of recorded time,
And all our yesterdays have lighted fools
The way to dusty death. Out, out, brief candle.
Life's but a walking shadow, a poor player
That struts and frets his hour upon the stage,
And then is heard no more. It is a tale
Told by an idiot, full of sound and fury,
Signifying nothing. (5.5.16–27)

For more sound and fury, Gerard Manley Hopkins is your
man. The nineteenth-century Jesuit priest jammed as many
sound effects as he could into his poetry. His logic: the greater
the sonics, the greater the praise to God. If you like rap and
hip-hop, lose yourself in Hopkins' "Carrion Comfort"; see
below. If you already love "Carrion Comfort," find yourself
some non-misogynist rap and hip-hop; rediscover what you
think you know.

Not, I'll not, carrion comfort, Despair, not feast on thee;
Not untwist—slack they may be—these last strands of man
In me ór, most weary, cry *I can no more*. I can;
Can something, hope, wish day come, not choose not to be.
But ah, but O thou terrible, why wouldst thou rude on me
Thy wring-world right foot rock? lay a lionlimb against me? scan

With darksome devouring eyes my bruisèd bones? and fan,

O in turns of tempest, me heaped there; me frantic to avoid
    thee and flee?

Why? That my chaff might fly; my grain lie, sheer and clear.

Nay in all that toil, that coil, since (seems) I kissed the rod,

Hand rather, my heart lo! lapped strength, stole joy, would
    laugh, chéer.

Cheer whom though? the hero whose heaven-handling flung
    me, fóot tród

Me? or me that fought him? O which one? is it each one? That
    night, that year

Of now done darkness I wretch lay wrestling with (my God!)
    my God.

Pound said, "Poetry begins to atrophy when it gets too far from music." One can argue over the idea all day long in a seminar room, but on the ground the majority of contemporary poets, even allegedly experimental poets, sprinkle rhyme, assonance, and consonance as one would salt, randomly and without measure. Do a blind taste-test: listen to a handful of recent poems. The one with the most sonic effects will probably be the one you like the best. As with pasta sauces, the one will the highest quantity of salt will most often be the favorite.

Rhythm

Think of rhythm in terms of beats. Music. Dance. In the English language, the eternal beat is the iamb (da-DUM): ex-IST to-DAY. Its obverse is the heartbeat-like trochee (DUM-da): IN-stant PUD-ding. All other beat patterns are variations of the iamb trying to escape the iamb.

Parsing the language of rhythm itself can be fun. Is it weird that *iamb* is a trochee? And what's this thing termed a "trochaic inversion"? Wouldn't that simply be an iamb—a trochee turned around? Meter-speak isn't so straightforward. Trochaic inversion means putting a trochee in a spot where one might expect an iamb. This formulation is akin to talking about a "near miss" between two airplanes. A near miss is, in any case, a miss—a close call. But a near miss, in fact, may also imply something else: a crash. And what is a crash? Two planes that no longer miss each other.

If you have difficulty discerning the beat pattern of a particular word, try putting the em-PHA-sis on the wrong sy-LLA-ble. Emphasis, or what's called stress, is always there in English even if you're not paying any attention. And which syllable gets emphasis can be relative, depending not just on the word's natural stress pattern but on the word before and after it—the whole line. Even a single word can change its emphasis: *present* as a noun is an iamb, *present* as a verb is trochee.

If you have trouble hearing beats across lines, listen to the measured beats in hip-hop or rap songs. To visualize the pattern of rhymes and rhythms, find the song's "flow diagram"—a chart that some rappers use to parse out their lines. (Paul Edwards, author of *How to Rap*, has an easy to follow video, including the flow diagram, of Eminem's "Lose Yourself," a rap that, no matter whether you like it or not, employs more sonic techniques line to line than just about any other in the genre.)

The English teacher's word for patterned rhythm is "meter" and her word for examining meter is "scansion." You scan a poem to understand how beats affect meaning. If you want punch, for instance, try the double-stress of the spondee: FUCK ME? FUCK YOU! But there's more to punch than profanity. Here's the beginning of Wilfred Owen's World War I poem "Dulce et decorum est," with capital letters to indicate stresses:

BENT DOUble, like OLD BEGgars UNder SACKS,
KNOCK-KNEED, COUGHing like HAGS, we CURSED
   through SLUDGE,
TILL ON the HAUNTing FLARES we TURNED our BACKS
AND TOWARDS our DIStant REST beGAN to TRUDGE.

Those relentless spondees at the beginning of each line mimic the lines' contents: soldiers trudging through an atrocious mess. The details of the war scene, in other words, are displayed by the rhythm in conjunction with its "message."

Rhythm is a part of a poem's "form": not what but *how* something is being communicated. Rhythm is the way a line is delivered, as an actor delivers a line, or as a rapper emphasizes certain syllables or words. But there's no reason why form has to coincide with content. That's just one possibility. In fact, when form contrasts with content things often get more interesting. Even a casual listen to Stephen Merritt singing "The Cactus Where Your Heart Should Be" will reveal that the content (lyrics) is utterly goofy, but the form (rhythm, sound, melody) is solemn, wistful—the friction between the two yields a particular kind of sublimity.

Whether you're looking or listening for it or not, rhythm operates in free verse: there still are syllables, there still are beats. You don't have to count them, you don't have to know their odd Greek names, but it helps to listen for beats in lines and to stop when something strikes your ear. The variations are as important as the patterns.

The point of noticing rhythm is often in noticing where rhythm changes. If a poem begins in a consistent rhythm, does it ever loosen that rhythm? If so, where? That spot will likely indicate a shift in the poem's content—more or less drama, a turn toward a new scene or a revelatory moment. If a poem maintains a consistent rhythm throughout, the question is not *Why did the poet do that?* but rather *Why does the poem do that, i.e., what's the effect of a consistent rhythm in the world of the poem?*

Ezra Pound liked to say that contemporary poets had to "break the back" of our language's most consistent meter: the pentameter, the five-beat line. Some poets today might argue that we should put the pentameter back into prose that passes for a lot of our unstructured poetry. But if you look closely, pentameter has never left us.

Enjambment

Miss Susie had a steamboat,
The steamboat had a bell.
Miss Susie went to heaven
And the steamboat went to hell-
O, operator
Give me number nine
And if you disconnect me
I will kick you from
Behind the refrigerator…

The schoolyard rhyme Miss Mary (or Hello Operator) is a small piece of genius when you are a kid. There's nothing like the first time you play with the ends of those lines, their syntactic breaking. The first time, that is, you forgo end-stopped lines and allow the syntax to spill over into the next line. This is called enjambment.

Matthea Harvey's first book, *Pity the Bathtub Its Forced Embrace of the Human Form*, is filled with similar examples of the duplicity (doubleness) of enjambment:

Pity the bathtub its forced embrace of the human
Form may define external appearance but there is room
For improvement within try a soap dish that allows for
Slippage is inevitable as is difference in the size of

The word "human" seems to be a noun in the first line, but after your eye moves to the second line, "human" becomes an adjective describing "form." The word is syntactically part of both lines at once. These "hard" enjambments, or as Harvey once termed them "lines ending with swivel words," illustrate how one line can be played against the next in a delightful, often ambiguous, friction.

If enjambment can elicit delight over lines, it can do so over stanzas. Notice the movement from one stanza to the next in Terrance Hayes' "Ode to Big Trend":

That's how Big Trend looked. There was a pink scar
Meddling his forehead. Most people assumed a bear

Like him couldn't read anything but a dollar,
But I'd watched him tour the used bookstore
In town and seen him napping so I knew he held more

Than power in those hands. They could tear
A Bible in two. Sometimes on the walk home I'd hear

Him reciting poems …

If you read only the first stanza here, you think that Big Trend got his scar from a bear. When you reach the second stanza, you realize "bear" refers back to Big Trend. And at the end of the second stanza, it feels like "more" might refer back to "dollar," as in "more dollars"—two words linked by their rhyme. But by the rules of syntax, "more" gets pulled into the first line of the third stanza: "more // Than power in those hands." And what does the speaker hear in the third stanza? It appears to be a bible being torn … until the speaker (and the reader) reaches the fourth stanza … and what's heard are "poems."

Intriguing, bold, affected, subtle, multifarious enjambments can be found all over contemporary poems. In fact, the most significant technical innovation in poetry in the last century is not the incorporation of vernacular or colloquial speech patterns ("language of the people or the street"), but the stylized use of the line break which has replaced the position that end rhyme and metrics once held.

The Line

Close study of how one line ends and moves into the next is as good as any entry point in examining a poem.

In addition to and apart from sentences and stanzas—*the line* demands to be examined on its own, with its own sense, as a *poetic unit.*

> Here is the little desk at which Napoléon played
> with his mother's necklace. There is the schoolbag
> Napoléon filled with broken seashells. Here is the sestina
> Napoléon couldn't finish. There is the delicate pastry
> on which Napoleon floated into the future …

This droll little text would appear to be prose arbitrarily broken up into lines—a criticism of many contemporary poems. But before we come to that conclusion, try actually writing out the text in prose, margin to margin, to see what's gained, what's lost:

Here is the little desk at which Napoléon played with his mother's necklace. There is the schoolbag Napoléon filled with broken seashells. Here is the sestina Napoléon couldn't finish. There is the delicate pastry on which Napoleon floated into the future …

The second version seems to lose little in meaning—they are the same words after all. But close inspection of *the lines* of the first version reveals something else. For just a moment in the line "Napoléon filled with broken seashells. Here is the sestina," it's intimated that the sestina is being filled with broken seashells by Napoléon. Of course, the period in the middle of the line tells us otherwise, but the line still shapes our thinking. A similar phenomenon happens in the line "Napoléon couldn't finish. There is a delicate pastry"—we know that Napoléon couldn't finish the sestina from the previous line, but for a second we think it's the pastry that Napoléon couldn't finish. This kind of work may strike you as too trifling, too subtle—it is. It also forges the line that separates poetry from prose, the poet from the prose writer.

Breaking bad prose into lines of poetry won't make the bad prose that much better. (Some poets are failed prose writers, but so are most prose writers.)

The Lyric

A lyric attempts to harness a particular moment, feeling, or experience. Originally, lyrics were accompanied by a lyre and told in the first person. Picture a musician on stage singing a tune while playing acoustic guitar. An epic attempts to capture a whole life or an age. It's the tall tale told around a campfire. Shorthand: lyric is short song; epic is a very long story. Combinations follow. Wordsworth and Coleridge tried blending the two in their *Lyrical Ballads*, and Whitman invoked himself instead of a muse at the beginning of his epic of the self in *Leaves of Grass*. In the twentieth century, many poets tried to blow both apart—into lyrical fragments that pointed to stories that were never really there.

Think of the lyric not as capturing a moment as a photograph does, but as the light itself that allows a photograph to be taken. What is the moment like before the photograph is taken, and after it is taken? And where is it taken to?

"Verse" can refer to an entire poem or to a single line of poetry. It comes to us from *versus* (Latin) meaning "to turn"—the ancient metaphor is of turning soil, plowing. Lines of verse can be thought of lines of crops: things you plant and cultivate in a field—a "field of text" or "text field." Think of the whole page, therefore, as your acreage.

```
H O R S
E I N T
R U C K
```

```
B I R D
I N P L
A N E
```

```
J A C
K I N
J I L L
```

```
L   Y
R I C
I S M
```

Metaphor

The Greek origin of *metaphor* is *transfer*. Metaphors are supposed to take you from one place to another. Buses in Athens are called *metaphorai*.

All language in fact is metaphoric. If you take in something with your senses, it usually gets processed into a voice in your head. *The bathroom stinks.* Sensory input has been transferred into a thought, a sentence, language.

That boy is a bug. Is it a transfer? It's really a substitution, or if you prefer an equation: boy = bug. *That boy is* like *a bug.* It's no longer a full substitution. Bug is superimposed over boy. The equation is now: boy $\cong$ bug.

If one accepts that metaphor is substitution, then what is one to do with T. S. Eliot's proposition that "Nothing in this world or the next is a substitute for anything else"? Metaphor, that is, becomes only a pseudo-substitution. Even two identical eggs aren't actually identical: one sits next to the other in the carton and they can be switched around, but the one is never materially the other. Metaphor is a kind of necessary deception that we accept mostly unthinkingly. So many of our thoughts are operational lies. The word "apple" stands in for the red-skinned, white-fleshed thing on the counter. And why is "apple" "apple"? Because there's an arbitrary system, made long ago and continually if incrementally changing, that's codified "apple" as "apple" not "orange," "banana," "dolphin," "hairball," "taxi," etc.

Since the origins of language cannot ever be fully known, we metaphorize its origin with the story of the Tower of Babel. But there's really no need. Apple is *pomme* in French, *sagar* in Basque, *apfel* in Dutch, яблоко in Russian, *olma* in Uzbek, etc. If there were something inherently connecting the word with the thing, then there would only be one human language.

The fact that there isn't one language, or one-to-one substitution between languages, makes language-play that much more pliable and exciting. As a beginning student of German can tell you, for example, the same morphological word g-i-f-t means "poison" in German. And when you dig a bit deeper, you find that in Old English gift means the "price of a wife" as in a dowry. Maybe Robert Frost's dictum that "poetry is what gets lost in translation" has merit, but isn't there more to be gained?

The point of examining figurative language isn't simply to be able to pick out a metaphor or simile from the line-up of a sentence. The point is to absorb and inhabit the concept that all language is playful and in play.

What a wicked slogan for Louisiana's state penitentiary, yes? Well, no. This was actually once the logo for a hospital in New Orleans.

For a good reader, metaphor will sooner or later become an incurable illness.

Ambiguity

The dog chased the cat with sharp teeth. Did the cat have the sharp teeth, or did the dog have them? *Never strike a child with your hand.* Does that mean it's okay to strike the kid with a stick? The English teacher will write "unclear" or "ambiguous" in the margins. But that's precisely the intent of many poems: to discomfit sensible thinking in order to provide an alternative sense.

Do you see a lovely young lady or an ugly old woman?

On the facing page, do you see a duck or a rabbit? Find one and then the other. Now try to see *both at the same time.* That's a kind of ambiguity: where two opposing concepts can be held in the mind simultaneously without "having to reach for either one"— Keats' "negative capability." It's a little circus trick for the mind, as

the Shakespeare scholar Stephen Booth says. It's also what a poem is best suited to do as compared to other kinds of writing.

And now, once you see one (the young woman or the old woman, the rabbit or the duck), try to see *neither*. That too is ambiguity. Which manifests in paradox, cognitive dissonance, oxymoron, aporia, *différence*, etc. All ways of describing the experience of putting a reader in an ostensibly uncomfortable position. Stuck in thought that appears to halt any other thought.

Because I could not stop for Death —
He kindly stopped for me —

Emily Dickinson's speaker's casual, even quaint, date with the grim reaper begins with a deceptively simple moment of ambiguity. Does the speaker not stop for Death because she is in too much of a hurry? Or is "because" to be understood in another sense, as in "on account of" or "for"—the speaker presumably not ready to die? And what's the sense of "for me"—does Death only stop "on account of" the speaker, not the other way around?

> The Carriage held but just Ourselves —
> And Immortality.

Even her ubiquitous dash is ambiguous: the dash severs as well as joins terms and phrases. If the carriage holds "just," as in only, "Ourselves," how do we logically deal with the "and" after the line break? The dash links and cuts off the two lines: at once "Ourselves" are with and without "Immortality." The severing and joining can't be completely separated—the ambiguity is held there in the reader's mind. Think of the dash the next time you slice a tomato: for a brief moment the knife (the dash) both cuts the tomato and connects its two severed pieces together.

It's been argued that because Dickinson used dashes in her poems as well as in her cake recipes, the dashes don't mean anything or aren't particular to her poems. But this only proves that while she baked—and she did so almost daily—she wrote poems and that she viewed a poem as a sort of recipe. On the back of her neighbor's coconut cake recipe is the draft of her poem that begins "The Things that never can come back, are several."

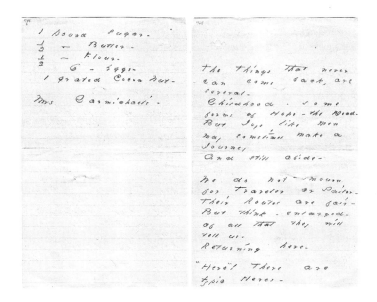

Dickinson

Had she published a book, her biographical note might have read: *Emily Dickinson divides her time between the kitchen and the bedroom.*

A framed portrait of Elizabeth Barrett Browning hung in Dickinson's bedroom. It may or may not have been the first thing she saw upon waking.

Dickinson should not be admired because someone says you should admire her. And her poems should not be regarded by who she was purported to be: a virgin, a recluse.

She made gingerbread for kids in the neighborhood and exchanged cooking tips with friends. She liked to doodle. She referred to her poems as needlework. She wrote lines and phrases and poems on anything she could find—newspaper scraps, receipts, wrapping papers, invitations, used envelopes. She grew indoor and outdoor gardens. She sent letters that included poems, and often letter and poem were indistinguishable. Upon her death, her sister discovered forty booklets, two-hole punched and bound with string, in which Dickinson had organized more than 800 of her poems.

The Complete Poems of Emily Dickinson is hard going at first, and it will not grow on you. You will grow into it as you age and continue reading. Like many great books, it is the very opposite of a page-turner.

Classics

A classic is a classic because of tradition and convention—nothing more. If we all lived in geodesic domes, we'd think that four walls and a roof was a radical innovation.

Never feel ashamed for not having read a classic. A majority
of poet-professors have never read a majority of the esteemed
works, whether Aristotle's *Poetics* or The Bible or the *Kama Sutra*
or the *I Ching*.

Never lie about having read a classic. This is tricky because you
are apt to lean on the generalizations or positions that others,
especially writers, have made. Which means that you can't really
discuss a classic you have not read except to quote what others
have said about it.

Sappho's lyrics have come down to us almost all in remnants.
Anne Carson's translation *If Not, Winter* uses brackets […] to
indicate missing, gapped, or failed sections of papyrus. The
result is a new, mad-libs Sapphic in which time and chance
have authored the poems as much as Sappho has … the work
suddenly ancient, contemporary, and experimental all at
once.

Curses, spells, complaints, prayers, chants—they arrived long
before formalized lyrics and epics. And that stuff we call iambic
poetry? It was originally not iambic at all. Iambic poetry, or
iambus, was a genre of poetry for rants, often obscene. And
iambic meter, if used, was considered unsophisticated because

it was closest to the rhythm of natural speech—to the ordinary citizen.

Instead of *The Odyssey* and *The Iliad*, begin your epic reading with *Gilgamesh*. Homer's stories may have the greater influence on Western literature, but the Mesopotamic tale predates them by more than a thousand years. *Gilgamesh* involves greater surrealism and fantasy, and features a grand love between two men, Gilgamesh and Enkidu, that is more tragicomic than homoerotic. Gilgamesh quests for eternal life; Odysseus just wants to get back home.

There's no need to finish reading an epic poem that you only got halfway through. Its purpose was to be read halfway.

Ancient poets cribbed from any source they could find, gathering the best parts in an effort to live a better life. In Early Modern Europe, the best classics were scrapbooks, called commonplace books, that were crammed with quotes, poems, letters, prayers, tables, facts and figures—all kinds of tidbits of useful information. Do not rely on others' packaging, or social media trending. Make your own commonplace book, or vade mecum, and call it *The Classics* or *The Waste Land* or *Tender Buttons*, if you like; book titles are not subject to copyright.

Myths

It may very well be that there was no Homer as such, nor an original *Odyssey* or *Iliad*. No matter. A brook comes babbling in; you enjoy its song even if its source is unknown.

In Ancient Greece drama began elementally, with sex and violence, the art and entertainment of a vase hurled between a man and a woman and another man. Or it didn't at all. The conceptions of ancient times are conceptions long after the fact. We perceive the ancients as ancient. There is no special irony in the fact that Horace, an ancient to us, argued for reading and studying contemporary poetry over ancient poetry.

In the Legends of King Arthur, the Holy Grail was something of a misnomer. Something knights went out looking for because there wasn't anything else to do in Camelot, except stare at the rain.

Myths exist to explain things we can't explain. For example, why is the sky so high? One African myth has it that the sky actually used to hang low enough to touch. But then people began using the sky as a napkin, making a mess of it, and so God moved it far out of reach.

Whitman and Dickinson. The two mothers of U.S. poetry. The gay man of the streets and the virgin in the attic. Both childless and isolated in their own rights, and yet they are the two myths that bind us.

Ninety percent of all myths are about loss. Ninety percent of all loss is about myth.

Great Books

When you come to William Blake, make sure to read the facsimile copies of his poems that include his illustrations. The illustrations don't illustrate, as such; they are part of the content and form of the work. For example, Blake's "The Tyger" takes on a special effect in the facsimile. He's a pussy-cat tiger, cartoonish, full of the rainbow. The images are suddenly at odds with the words. Therein you can re-envision the lesson of Blake's contraries: his bright, fearful symmetries.

The canon of great poems can be bought anywhere; build your own anthology of almost great ones.

In 1850, Elizabeth Barrett Browning published a collection entitled *Sonnets from the Portuguese*. The forty-four poems, in fact, were not translated from Portuguese and have nothing to do with Portugal. The title was invented to prevent readers from relying on the poet's biography to explain the poems—which many cite as the first acclaimed love poems from a woman's point of view. Initially, the book's title was *Sonnets from the Bosnian*.

August 7, 1853. How trivial and uninteresting and wearisome and unsatisfactory are all employments for which men will pay you money! The ways by which you may get money all lead downward. To have done anything by which you earned money merely is to have been truly idle. If the laborer gets no more than the wages his employer pays him, he is cheated, he cheats himself. Those services which the world will most readily pay for, it is most disagreeable to render. You are paid for being something less than a man. The state will pay a genius only for some service which it is offensive to him to render. Even the poet-laureate would rather not have to celebrate accidents of royalty.

Dangle-berries have begun.

What a passionate, quasi-Romantic, Marxian brief ... suddenly undercut by berries! Skip Thoreau's classroom classics *Walden* and *Civil Disobedience* and move right to his *Journal*. It's filled with innumerable passages like the above, illustrating the power of juxtaposition, unexpectedness, and even, dare we say it about Thoreau: comedy. The two million words he wrote over twenty-five years have never been published in their entirety; but

Damion Searls has edited the best abridged version, at 650 pages, available from New York Review Books.

Sourcing dozens of works, from Homer and Dante and Baudelaire to the Bible and the Upanishads and Celtic mythology, T. S. Eliot's *The Waste Land* confronts the past admirably—and loses. Although it is a baggy monster of bricolage, the poem has great utility as a demonstration of collaboration; witness Ezra Pound's edits (mostly strike-outs), in the facsimile edition, that midwifed Eliot's final version. Moreover, it is a fine example of a poem-as-project; those pages of sometimes helpful, sometimes baffling author's "Notes"— included because one of Eliot's publishers believed the poem too short to publish as its own book—are as much a part of the poem as the body of the poem itself.

An under-taught American classic *The Life of Poetry* by Muriel Rukeyser traces the sources, fears, and uses of poetry *outside* of the poetry world. "Art is action," she writes, "but it does not cause action; rather, it prepares us for thought." This is the thought manual for the poet who wants her art to be uniquely unnecessary.

Although Frank O'Hara is best known for his allegedly ad-hoc "I do this, I do that" poems, he should be better known as the twentieth century's foremost love poet. Keep his *Collected Poems* on the nightstand; the next time you have an issue with a poet or lover in bed, open the book at random and begin reading. If you need quick redemption, try "Poem" (p. 41) or "For Grace, After a Party" (p. 214) or "Having a Coke with You" (p. 360).

Who is the most underrated poet in the English language? Longfellow? Mina Loy? An unknown garment worker in an unknown factory in New York City, 1928? No. The answer is always: William Shakespeare.

Whitman

On the following page is the frontispiece of the first edition of *Leaves of Grass* (1855), a book that included the author's name not on the cover or in the front matter, but only once, about 500 lines into the book: "Walt Whitman, an American, one of the roughs, a kosmos …"

Hat cocked, arm akimbo, collar spread open—undo that second button of the shirt and he looks more pimp than poet. Pimp's neither apocryphal nor far off. The speaker in *Leaves of Grass* pimps himself out—not merely taking on the voice of others, as one expects in a dramatic monologue, but merging with others—

"I am the hounded slave"—and even replacing others—"I turn the bridegroom out of bed and stay with the bride myself, / And tighten her all night to my thighs and lips."

From the beginning Whitman's speaker seeks to merge with you, dear reader: "For every atom belonging to me as good belongs to you." And by the end he wants you, if not to merge, then at least to identify, with those he has tirelessly catalogued in the poem, both living and dead:

> Great are Yourself and Myself,
> We are just as good and bad as the oldest and youngest or any,
> What the best and worst did, we could do,
> What they felt, do not we feel it in ourselves?
> What they wished, do we not wish the same?

You might conceptualize *Leaves of Grass* as *The Great American Poem*—the answer to Emerson's essay "The Poet" calling for a new poetry of the American idiom. Whitman himself hoped his book would become a present-day bible for the masses. For all the commentary one can read about the work—it's breaking of tradition in content (inclusive of the ordinary or the lowly both in body and society) and in form (the gangling free verse lines), it now simply seems to be a long lyric sustained by a series of questions—more than two hundred in all—the most central being *What is the grass?*

Leaves of Grass... shouldn't it be "blades" of grass? Closely read. "Leaves" point to the object of the book itself: each page a leaf, and each leaf a page composed of what was once a tree. "Composed," Whitman's speaker might say, "of me."

When you go back to re-read the book's first section, you begin to feel it's a misnomer. "Song of Myself" turns out to be paradoxically, hubristically "Songs of Others" and then "Songs of Everyone and Everything." The more one listens to Whitman's speaker, the more one agrees with him but is less interested in him. In too much agreement there is boredom.

While reading a long poem, such as *Leaves of Grass*, it's invaluable to fall asleep periodically. Those moments between waking and sleeping are fertile, portentous spaces for the imagination.

The deacon, the duck-shooter, the squaw, the deckhand, the Kentuckian, the quadroon girl, the coon-seeker, etc.—the tallying and embodying of as many individuals and levels of society as the speaker can name. You can grow disgusted by the performance. But then you come across Allen Ginsberg's "A Supermarket in California," written exactly a hundred years later (the poem's last line "—*Berkeley, 1955*"), in which Whitman is wonderfully, ironically described as a "childless, lonely old grubber" and a "lonely old courage-teacher," and you are sympathetic all over again to his ingratiating transcendence.

Imagery

Ever since Modernism, people have talked about imagery dominating poetry—pictures doing all the hard work and a poem's euphony as mere karaoke, an orchestra emptied.

Imagery begins with a noun: a person, place, or thing. *There is the doctor.* Don't you see a man? *There is the nurse.* Don't you see a woman? Imagery is more complicated than seeing an image alone: the doctor and the nurse could be a woman and a man or two men or two women. Denotations demand connotations. *The girl is nursing.* Who's nursing whom?

They say to use all your five senses when you write poems, traditionally defined as: seeing, hearing, tasting, smelling, touching. *Do you hear that chickadee?* No, you see in your mind a small bird, a member of the tit family. A birdwatcher might tell you that that bird's call sounds like this: *cheeeeese-bur-ger, cheeeeese-bur-ger.* Did that sound make you see a patty of ground-up cow, painted with an orange square of its mother's coagulated milk, resting between two whole-wheat buns? Imagery entails more than images and their descriptors. And our senses? A neuroscientist would advance that there are far more than five, such as proprioception, or that sensory inputs are far more complex, such as echo-location, or that there's only one sense: touch. Smell is simply molecules touching other molecules in nasal passages, sight is simply light signals touching the rods and cones of the retina, etc.

Try viewing a poem as Roland Barthes does a photograph—using his *studium* and *punctum*. Studium is your immediate or overall impression: *I like it/I don't like it.* Punctum is where the poem—frequently with its images—first pricks, stings, or otherwise strikes you—positively or negatively.

To think of a poem in photographic or cinematic terms would initially seem like a good idea—especially a lyric poem, one that, like a photograph, attempts to capture a moment. But closely read the idea. *Capture* a moment? Was the moment hostile, wild? Maybe all moments are hostile and wild? Maybe we should leave the eye of the camera to others. Photographs are anyway mostly cruel.

Williams Carlos Williams believed that only ordinary, plain diction and syntax should be used in a poem. No symbols, and especially no similes ("they're much too false"). But at the end of his life Williams wrote his major poem, "Asphodel," that included an assortment of metaphors, symbols, and even references concerning Homer's ship cataloguing and

Helen's well-composed face. This is just to say that Williams' plums and his wheelbarrow aren't simple things (objects in the world) at all; they are words. Constructs. His "no ideas but in things" is useful to get us thinking precisely about our images. But without the phrase "so much depends upon," the red wheelbarrow, the rainwater, and those chickens have little import; it's the scaffolding of rhetoric that gives them meaning.

Examine poems for their prepositions. Out, of, by, with, from, to, before, between, through, about, beside, etc. They provide the framework that holds images together. In your own poems where you have one preposition, try changing it out with a number of different prepositions, noticing each new effect and expectation.

A deer is a beautiful image. A baby deer is a more beautiful image. A baby deer freshly dead, decomposing is still more beautiful. But is it prettier to call that baby deer a fawn?

Put a name to that fawn.
Rodger?
A new image; comedic.
Bambi?
Now you've had it: the sentiment has turned sentimental.

Imagery takes practice, like playing nice with others, projection, transference, and any number of concepts a child psychologist has been made to memorize. Imagery sometimes requires one to concentrate very hard on, say, hanging onto someone's clammy hand while listening to a tall man deliver a brimstone lecture about a good book he's read only selectively. Imagery becomes, sooner or later, unruly and subterranean and moves against established patterns. In Steinian terms: *so that necessity is a silk under wear*.

Now look at this deer on the road, on p. 225, in Gabriel Gudding's *Rhode Island Notebook*:

> large dog or small deer
> 80W 318m 12:43pm
> Big deer 327m
>   After seeing this I
> wonder if it wd be possible to kill
> A deer using only a thumbtack.
> How many times wd I have to
> stab the deer w/ the thumbtack in
> order to kill it.

One tiny image makes another image larger, for all time; will you ever see a deer or a thumbtack the same way again?

Avoid talking about "symbolism" or "a symbol." It's a red herring—meaning, if you look for some kind of "idea" behind an image you tend to forget entirely about the image itself. In *The Great Gatsby*, that green light at the end of Daisy's dock is a green light first and foremost. It's not so much a "symbol" of anything as it is a thing patterned in the narrative—an object that appears at various times in the story, and links together other things (Daisy) and concepts (wealth, the American Dream). It may be a central or connecting image, but there's certainly nothing hidden behind it; everything is on the surface if you know how piece it together.

Which is lonelier: an empty field or a field in which stands a single tree? Neither. You are the lonely one, and your loneliness illustrates what's known as the pathetic fallacy: projecting human feelings onto things that aren't human.

Roses

Once upon a time a nightingale fell in love, sang a song to the point of delirium, to the point of accidentally on purpose thrusting its breast against the thorn of a rose, bleeding all over the bud, turning it forever red and platonic in our eyes.

A rose is a rose is a rose. The infamous and under understood phrase from Gertrude Stein. A rose is clearly not a rose. "Rose" is a word standing in for that flowery thing that is out there in the garden. To say "a rose is a rose" is already once removed from what a rose really is.

A rose is a rose is a rose. Does the rose turn a deeper red when it's repeated three times? Perhaps. But couldn't the rose also fade with such wear? The repetition of rose makes the rose less of a rose and more of a piece of language. Say it again aloud: *a rose is a rose is a rose*. Did you detect it? *Arose*: to ascend. Stein's phrase isn't about making the rose more rosy, but how language takes on a life of its own.

In case you have questions about how many roses to send your beloved, the kind folks at Teleflora, a clearinghouse for florists, provides a system of answers. A single rose means love at first sight. Three roses is for the one-month anniversary. Six signals infatuation. Ten: perfect love. A dozen: be mine. Fifteen: an apology. Twenty: "my feelings for you are truly sincere." Two dozen: "shouts 'I'm yours!'" Three dozen: "I'm head over heals!" Fifty: "a love that knows no bounds"…just like the artist Jay DeFeo's one-ton, ten-foot-tall, seven-years-in-the-making painting entitled "The Rose," which looks nothing like a rose, Teleflora provides a rose with a life it never wanted.

Once the petals fall off, Stein might have said, all metaphor is disgusting.

Prose Poetry

"Prose poetry" would seem a contradiction in terms—potentially a fine ambiguity—but often a prose poem boils down to a piece of prose that someone simply calls a poem. It is also known here and there as micro-fiction, flash fiction, lyrical prose, and short-shorts.

Prose poems are, for the most part, more prose than poetry—that is, they are structured more along the lines of story and scene than song.

Baudelaire's *Paris Spleen* and Rimbaud's *Illumination*s are usually credited with inventing the form, but there may be no better place to begin examining the prose poem than by comparing Genesis 1:1–2:3 and Genesis 2:4–3:24. And no place better to end one's examination than with trying to determine if the last line of Borges' "Argumentum Ornithologicum" is possible. For what comes in between the Bible and Borges, read Melville's *Moby-Dick*—a text that could serve in place of any canonical poetry anthology.

Instead of studying prose poems, study the workings of prose itself—character and event and plot—in the novel or the memoir. Eschew the short story, the most difficult genre even if young writers often start with it. As in a poem, every sentence counts in a short story, but there are too many possible scenarios of character, scene, and event to manage for a beginner.

Studying the short story mostly gets you sucked into writing a short story, and writing a short story takes too much time for what it's worth, perhaps a publication in a journal which few will bother to read.

The novel is the most capacious, forgiving form—one can put nearly anything in it without breaching the borders esotericism. Or rather the novel was made for esotericism. Haruki Murakami's *The Wind-Up Bird Chronicle* is a strangely beautiful novel that includes not a single paragraph one might be obligated to call a prose poem.

A prose poem is really a failed attempt at lineating a poem, or is a piece of prose that has failed to turn into a longer work. Like Montaigne's *Essays*, which are literally "attempts" or "trials," prose poems illustrate that there is nothing wrong with a failure of form.

If the prose poem does nothing else, it illustrates that even straightforward prose is affected prose.

Narrative

Story, or more accurately narrative, is what we use both consciously and unconsciously to guide our lives. We try to fit everything—from our eating habits to our reading habits—into a narrative. But not every poem has to tell a story. Just as not every vehicle has to have four wheels, or even must be in motion.

Please do not story-fuck a poem: cherry-picking a few details or lines in order to service the story you wish the poem told. Similarly, be careful of your *own* story—that is, of having to make the poem fit into the story you're telling yourself today.

Narrative poetry tells a story. A story involves a character(s) who experiences a series of events: beginning, middle, end. Though a narrative may not tell them in that order (cf. *in medias res.*) A narrative traces the way events tie into each other (pattern-up), which is called plot. You closely read plot in the same way you closely read images, sonics, etc. Look for patterns and variations on those patterns.

Narrative appears to give a linear structure to what appears to be chaos. Lyric is the phenomenon of appearance—the attempt to inhabit a timeline by picking out a single point on it.

They will tell you that literature is all about telling stories that aim to get you to understand what it's like to be someone else. They are not wrong; they just haven't watched enough videos.

We tell ourselves stories not only because stories are entertaining, but because we believe that stories will make death less unthinkable. We create a narrative arc for our memories, our lives, so that we can die with a modicum of integrity. So that we can say "I accomplished something, good or bad, I was here, and now I say goodbye." But such storytelling is only one version of the events of a life.

The last act of a narrative may be to recast all that has been told before into the coffin, the plot, and headstone. It may also be to turn its back on narrative altogether, burned up and ashed—to fragment, to scatter, to return to nowhere.

A cultural need for story comes from a personal need for things, ultimately everything, to come to an end that seems desirable to end on. Which is why the apocalypse is so attractive: it promises that all stories would end the same and there would be only one story left to tell.

Criticism and Theory

It would seem that a literary critic's job is to fight against literary quality that is determined by quantification. Best seller's lists, mass-produced thrillers, mysteries, romance novels, and self-help guides. The labels "Best" and "Great" are shorthand for what has been published (not necessarily read) the most over the greatest amount of time.

Do not fear literary critics; they are just woodpeckers. The more diseased the tree, the happier they are.

Analyzing literature quantitatively, as Franco Moretti does in his "distant reading," is useful in understanding historical contexts and trends—as long as one remembers that a poem is big data disguised as little data.

You will gain a greater understanding of a poem by writing a single parody of it than by reading nine-tenths of the literary criticism around it. This is why some of the best literary criticism is in fact parody.

Two illustrious literary theorists sit at a table. The first theorist states his theory about X. The second theorist restates the first theorist's theory about X and is about to attack X when the first theorist says that the second theorist doesn't even have X restated properly. The second theorist complains that he's written an entire book about X exactly as he's stated it. The first theorist rests his case. The second grimaces like a hostile witness. The audience goes wild with sighs.

Consumerism consumes language. (What else would it do?) Amazon. Coach. Saturn. Twitter. Words shifted from their original meanings—in both denotation and connotation. Would the world be more just if more companies would abstain from co-opting existing words and instead invent new ones—like Häagen-Dazs, Lego, Prius, and Wii? Would the titles of poems equally benefit from such practice?

You don't have to Foucault, Deleuze, or Cixous to understand that language hijacks other language. The point is pointless: language is ludic. And so should any serious understanding of poetry be.

Feel free to view a poem through any of the Isms—Classicism, Confucianism, Humanism, Romanticism, Marxism, Structuralism,

Historicism, Post-Colonialism, etc. Be careful, though, not to limit your view to only one of these filters, you're sure to get blindsided.

Derrida is the existentialist of language. His concept of free or infinite play (*joue*) doesn't mean there's a lack of meaning in, say, a poem, but rather an abundance of it. Not *nothing* matters, but *everything* does. Deconstruction is an affirmation of language not a withering of it.

Deconstruction admits that humans, not god(s), created language. Nietzsche is important not only because he pointed out that humans made up God and then forgot that they made him up, but because what follows of this understanding: that humans made up everything else, too. It's not that God is dead; He was never alive.

The notion that a poem is a construct is, of course, a construct. There's no looking outside of the system of language without language. As soon as you describe a thing, for example, it's no longer that thing—it's merely a description of that thing. As soon as you have a linguistic representation of the spirit, the spirit's lost. Which is why in *The Book of Exodus*, God gets the most poetic, most ambiguous of names: I AM THAT I AM. A name that is supposed to be no name.

Might Slavoj Žižek's greatest contribution to literary theory be that literary theory best be classified as manifesto, for which coffee mugs can be made and T-shirts printed?

Any poetic movement—from Symbolism and Imagism to Confessionalism and Flarfism—will live only as long as someone wants to teach it to others. The poems in and of those movements themselves are artifacts—without authorities (poets, teachers, scholars) to recover them they might as well have never existed.

Post-Modernism (or Po-Mo) has been confused by critics and laypeople alike for decades. The situation is clear: Po-Mo isn't a turning away from or improvement on Modernism (Mo); Po-Mo is simply what came after Mo, and almost everything that's attributed to Po-Mo is already present in Mo. Texts without a central meaning (logos)? Check. Mashed-up texts, intertextuality? Check, check. Multiple authors, texts sans authors, found or erasured texts? Triple check. Texts that aren't even texts. Checkmate. Mo cut the patterns, Po-Mo produces the variations.

Let's not get carried away with meta-politeness. Literary theory is simply another kind of literature. It is as much philosophy as the warning on a package of nuts: *May Contain Nuts*. It is as much pornography as devouring a cashew the shape of a lover's dimple. It is as much eulogy as one can compose for a zit. Would that real life were so simple.

Pessoa

If you had to get stranded on an island with a single Modernist, you could choose no one better than Fernando Pessoa—mainly because he wasn't just any one: he was multiple ones. The island would suddenly populate into a small village. Pessoa, which means "person" in Portuguese, created heteronyms (more than seventy) that weren't simply pseudonyms; they were fully fleshed out authors who had entire biographies (including astrological charts), wrote in wildly variegated styles, and argued with each other in magazines. The heteronyms became so real to Pessoa that he sabotaged his only in-person romantic relationship (with Ophelia Queiroz, a secretary in his office) by repeatedly letting one of his other selves write her letters that disparaged Fernando Pessoa.

Pessoa might be called the Whitman and Dickinson of Portugal. His poems possess Dickinsonian first lines (e.g., "Pack your bags for Nowhere at All!"; "Not only wine but oblivion I pour."), and his prose runs Whitmanesque in its discursive exuberance and transcendence (e.g., "How much I die if I feel for everything! How much I feel if I wander this way, disembodied and human, with my heart motionless like a beach, and the entire sea of everything, in the night in which we live, in a fury, striking the shore, and growing cold in my eternal, nocturnal stroll along the seaside!"). But the Whitman-Dickinson formulation is merely a convenient opinion. Pessoa's multitudes—labyrinthine, melancholic, self-annihilating—can't be contained. At his death in 1935, at age forty-seven, Pessoa left a trunk of 30,000 pages of scrawled texts that scholars are still happily sifting through and deciphering.

Zoom in on Pessoa and his work and all goes blurry. He wasn't really a Modernist—at least not in the ways of Pound, Eliot, Stein, or Williams. He wasn't even a Post-Modernist, for that would simply describe a handful of qualities of his works: fragmentary, intertextual, metafictional, maximal, minimal, authorless, etc. As a label, in other words, post-modern is insufficient. Pessoa deconstructed his life as he was living it—a means of personal survival—decades before Derrida would come to describe the notion.

Political Poetry

All poetry is political. But is it any more so than other formulations of the English language? Consider the diction of our grammar: subject and object. A sentence involves a power relationship, and politics by definition is a struggle for or management of power. For example, I AM THAT I AM is a battle for self-control.

When Theodor Adorno said "To write poetry after Auschwitz is barbaric," he wasn't calling for poets to stop writing; he was calling for them to write with the barbarism of the Holocaust always in the back of their minds—for every poet to bear witness to the barbarism around them. What happened instead was the creation of an entire subgenre called "witness poetry."

Poets aren't in the business of predicting the future, but they can prophesize. True prophets, that is, don't foresee the future, they point out what needs changing, what others are ignoring, in the present. They are not oracles; they are exposed nerves.

The precursor of witness poetry is Charles Reznikoff's *Testimony: The United States (1885–1915)*, a 500-page, two-volume collection of poems that details human injustice, suffering, violence—all sculpted from court records, and all without names. Reznikoff's later work *Holocaust* is similarly fashioned—drawing on survivors' testimonies from the Eichmann and Nuremberg trials. Some argue that the genius of these works is in allowing the facts and details to speak for themselves—unadorned and unrefined by the usual stratagems of poetry. Others argue the opposite—that the facts are only the starting points for getting readers to empathize—or that the facts as they are presented are not "just the facts," having been selected and edited down by their maker.

Readers, even the most attentive, are now so accustomed to poetry of witness that virtually any poem about a real war is easily dismissed or classified as "war" or "witness" or "protest" poetry. The phenomenon parallels the segregation of poetries at the end of the twentieth century: queer poetry, spoken-word poetry, indigenous poetry, etc. These poetries are now well known not for their sentiments or forms or experiments but for their categorization. The categorization has, sadly, become the whole of the sentiment.

Not all poets are visionaries but all poets can be subversives, even if they are subverting only their own visions periodically.

A great deal of political poetry borrows the techniques of new journalism: the non-oppressed visit the oppressed in foreign lands (foreign also meaning simply "different") and report back not only what and who they've seen but how their seeing affected what and who they've seen. The poet inserts his or her lyric "I" into the public spaces of others; one might more frankly call this disaster porn.

Shelley claimed that "poets are the unacknowledged legislators of the world." But what do poets enact—emotional laws? It's a futile debate. Numerous potential poets today go into advertising, marketing, speech-writing, digital media content-making. What's left to a poet is what's left to all of us: our economics. In late capitalism, consumers are the unacknowledged legislators, even if we mostly legislate unconscious of what we buy, from whom, and why.

The ancients understood that satire was invaluable; they made the satiric a form right alongside the lyric and the epic. But today satire, comedy, absurdity, and tragicomedy all tend to get overlooked as strategies for political poems. As we know from other media—such as Jon Stewart's *The Daily Show* or David Rees' comic series *Get Your War On*, or from performances by

Chris Rock, Margaret Cho, Louis C.K.—comedy doesn't have to be for entertainment only.

Far too many political poems trade exclusively in solemnity and earnestness: they preach to a choir whose ears are tired of the tune. But it doesn't have to be. "Poetry is the ultimate vessel for comedy," as the poet Gabriel Gudding writes, "because of its pretentiousness, lofty status and distance from the masses."

"What is comedy?" asks the Rabbi.

"A joke?" says the poet.

"Too easy."

"Schadenfreude?"

"Too German."

Poet and novelist Paul Beatty: "Save for ... a select groups [of writers] the defining characteristic of the African-American writer is sobriety—moral, corporeal, and prosaic ... African Americans, like any other Americans, are an angry people with fragile egos ... Sometimes you laugh to keep from crying. Sometimes you laugh to keep from shooting." In the words of another Beatty—Brian Beatty—"Laughter is the best medicine, and if you are a Christian Scientist, it is the only medicine."

Can a poem still matter outside of a poem-world? In 2013, Patricia Lockwood's poem "Rape Joke," published in the online magazine *The Awl*, went viral generating more controversy and deep discussion about rape and feminism than pundits and scholars have been able to accomplish in decades. And the poem did it by being at once tragic and comedic.

Aesthetics

There is no accounting for taste. What one reader admires, another disdains. You will develop your likes and dislikes over time. This is called aesthetics.

One must develop one's aesthetics by reading magazines, books, and texts from the widest possible array of sources, from the *Song of Songs* to eighteenth-century French cookbooks, from West African folktales to Jean Toomer's *Cane*, from *Don Quixote* to Donna Tartt, from Philip Larkin to M. NourbeSe Philip, and from far wider, far beyond.

What's the relationship between aesthetics and ethics? Whatever the answer, don't pretend to have it all worked out. You're going to have to question others' motivations, biases, and notions of right and wrong as much and as deeply as your own.

Do not fully discount what you dislike. From time to time, continue to read what you dislike because it will help you remember why you like what you like. And over a long period of time some of your likes and dislikes will reverse. If they do not, your thoughts will stifle and your writing will be ruined.

Even if you are fond of a particular subgenre, say, Neo-Formalism or Conceptualism, you are still allowed to abhor aspects of it.

Don't pretend to love a poem you really find dull. Don't be afraid of disliking a great poem or a great poet. We all need villains. But praise poems that bore you; their crime is your thorn, and your thorn is your inspiration.

Certain classic poems are certain pills: reportedly good for you but hard to swallow. Never be afraid to crush a pill in order to get it down.

Regarding lists of the greatest poems of all time, critics will try to convince you that ranking is for experts and disappointment is for amateurs.

A new edition of *The Best American Poetry* comes out each year. There is the perennial "series" editor who selects the annual guest editor, and together they wield bolos cutting through the hundreds of thousands of poems published each year, so that we may re-relish America's penchant for all things in culture to be decidedly ranked. The book, it turns out, is useful in highlighting the aesthetics of one American, that guest editor (the Decider in David Foster Wallace parlance), and is only partially American since it excludes Central and South America. "Best" as a superlative would seem lightly molested by such serial endeavors, but that would be going too far. There are usually some very good poems in the collection; 1994 was a particularly fine year. Still, a more accurate title for the series would be something like *A Clutch of Unconcatenated Poems That a U.S. Poet Kinda Enjoyed in the Small Hours Before Drifting off to Sleep*.

Reader Response

My Papa's Waltz

The whiskey on your breath
Could make a small boy dizzy;
But I hung on like death:
Such waltzing was not easy.

We romped until the pans
Slid from the kitchen shelf;

My mother's countenance
Could not unfrown itself.

The hand that held my wrist
Was battered on one knuckle;
At every step you missed
My right ear scraped a buckle.

You beat time on my head
With a palm caked hard by dirt,
Then waltzed me off to bed
Still clinging to your shirt.

What's the intent of Theodore Roethke's poem? Is it a nostalgic scene in a kitchen between a father and child (mother looking on) who are horsing around after the father gets home from a hard day's work? Or, is it a scene that depicts something more sinister—thinly veiled child abuse—evidenced by the diction: whiskey, death, battered, scraped, beat, clinging? The interpretation you find more plausible will tell you as much about yourself as it does about the poem.

You read into a poem what you want to read. This is the same thing Thoreau admits doing as he walks through a field or forest; he sees what he wants to see, what is already inside himself: *The objects I behold correspond to my mood.* When on April 13, 1854, Thoreau notes in his journal that a man's body has been found in a river nearby, he writes: *How these events disturb our associations and tarnish the landscape! It is a serious injury done to a stream.*

Reading between the lines only means something if the lines are any good.

Often a reader expects a poem to fulfill a certain desire. If that desire goes unfulfilled, it is assumed that the poem has failed the reader when, in fact, the opposite is more likely to be true.

Classroom Reading

Reading a poem aloud in a classroom setting is sometimes uncomfortable. The teacher should make it more so. Fill the room with anxiety, create a circumstance where something will have to give, the pressure release, and everyone, including the teacher, can come to the poem from a new place—one that doesn't exist outside the classroom where the poem is merely another thing in the world.

Quaker Reading. Instead of asking (or begging) for a volunteer to read the poem, the teacher tells the class that they will all sit in silence until whoever feels moved to read the poem aloud reads the poem aloud. This is what Quakers call "unprogrammed worship." The longer the silence, the greater the expectancy and potential for being moved.

Invocation. Begin class with the recitation of a poem—not as a summoning of muses or poetry gods, but simply to mark the beginning of class from whatever came before. This is a chance for students to practice their oral skills. Let a different student chose the poem for each meeting. Any published poem—ancient to contemporary, well-known to unknown, any topic or style—between one and three pages. (Allowing students to bring in poems gives them some investment and obligation about seeking out poems, and it also gives the teacher a good opportunity to revisit poems she knows or to hear new ones.) Have the student read the poem aloud (no visible copy for anyone else); this is a chance to practice aural awareness. Afterwards, ask the class what they heard—what struck them about the poem or the reading—a specific line, image, sonic effect, or even just a word. If students are hesitant, have the student read the poem again. If it's a really short poem, maybe it's read three or four times. Sometimes discussion segues into the topic of the day—sonics or line breaks or metapoetics. Sometimes the poem's content lends itself to a poem previously examined in class. Sometimes the teacher may not like the poem. But she must accept it—must improvise—must allow it to be put into play.

The traditional classroom is, or can be, a refuge from civilization; it is one of the only surviving places you may feel unencumbered or even encouraged to daydream.

Poetry Readings

The way to really know how close you are to someone is to test the relationship to near destruction. Take him or her to a poetry reading.

A reading often feels like a little convention of loners who believe they should get out at least once a month. The event can produce anxiety and paradoxical feelings. The poems to be read have been made by an individual alone in a room, and are mostly read later alone in a room. But at a reading the room is suddenly filled with all these individuals. And if a few friends or family show, it's both private and public. The poet stands there like a stain on the wall, for people to inspect or pretend to ignore. The sticky spot of time is about to begin in which one reader will attempt to connect with, what was until a few moments earlier, a number of invisible readers.

A poetry reading serves a social function as much as it does a literary one, and therefore may benefit from hooking into other social events—school bazaars, co-op openings, gallery walks, playground constructions, farmer's markets, political protests, etc. But the most communal readings take place with poet-friends in apartments and homes, in backyards, on front stoops and rooftops—where the poetical and the social merge organically, or later consensually on a blanket or in a bed.

Giving a poetry reading is not about your poetry; it's about playing the part of the poet. Since the image that the poem cuts on the page may not be able to be conveyed (its form often invisible to the ear), the poem's delivery becomes everything. Tone, timing, cadence, pitch, facial expression, posture, clothing, and even that glass of water on the podium. These are all now part of the poem, which itself becomes a prop.

Despite the potential for clinking glasses and background chatter, reading at a drinking establishment will always be more successful than reading at a bookstore. But bookstore readings still hold their literary history and allure: standing at a podium where other poets and writers once stood.

If after reading a poem at a poetry reading, the poet remarks *That one just wrote itself!*, don't fail to respond as my former student Hilary Gunnels once did: *And did it publish itself too?*

POET W/ CAPE.

Attending a poetry reading is like attending church: you might not look forward to the experience but you imagine it'll be good for the soul. Each time it ends, however, you swear you'll never again expose yourself to such simulated sentiment.

The greatest compliment one poet can give another after a reading is: *Damn you, I wish I had written that.*

Reader's Block

Even for a poet or teacher, reading poetry can become a phobia. The only way to get over it is to face it head-on. That may mean pressing your face to the page or the screen until you feel actual pain.

Find a poem you like and type it out—on a keyboard is fine, but on a manual typewriter is far better as your fingers will have to push harder, making the impression in your mind deeper. And there's nothing more satisfying than coming to the end of a line and knocking the carriage return back to the right to advance the paper, and having finished typing, turning the roller and pulling the poem out of the machine.

Keep your books in random places—on tables, chairs, window sills, between sofa cushions, among clothing in drawers, in the pantry, in the oven, in the car, in the shed—anywhere but on bookshelves where they will go untouched, obstacles to nothing.

A good reader does not know where she is going. A perfect reader does not know where she came from.

Some readers come to dislike a poem that talks about itself as a poem: what is sometimes referred to as a meta-poem or meta-poetics. Such resistance seems to be a failure of childhood. It's in innumerable children's books that we first apprehend books calling attention to their bookiness.

Spirituality

Poems are apparitions of what was once there, poised between piety and desire. They are mechanisms of suddenness that spring from a want for mystical or spiritual life. When you are standing in front of a river surging down a mountain, you don't think to yourself *I wonder what that means*. You simply take in the experience. But then you remember a line from a dead German poet... *beauty is nothing but the beginning of a terror that we are barely able to endure... every angel is terrible...*. These words conjure up his ghost, but that angel is all yours.

Proust said that reading only introduces us to spiritual life; it does not constitute it. Writing, he forgot to add, constitutes it.

Humans invented God because looking over the precipice of a cliff is both terrifying and exhilarating. But the unknown is a mystery too mysterious; the idea of God made the mysterious less so, and eventually prepared us for seeking out new mysteries— those of science. Poetry's mysteries, by comparison or contrast, have never left us.

The older one gets, the stranger God becomes. Poetry is a way of being estranged from the world, like the god one wishes to become.

Poetry, like all religions, has its spiritual problems. Christians must recall that the Lord and Jesus were united in a murder-suicide pact. Jews must recall that being the chosen people was their choice. Buddhists must recall that Buddha abandoned his wife and infant son to become Buddha. Atheists must recall that God has authored a book in which God doesn't exist.

Flight

Like air travel, reading connects you to others through space and time. Particularly on a plane there's absolutely little else to do that seems worthwhile besides reading. One can listen to music or watch a video, but those things are passive and one doesn't always want to feel so checked-out on a plane. Or rather, one wants feel checked-out in the right way. Staring out the porthole window at killer cumulous nimbi is utterly transcendent; it's also the ideal time to read poems.

Begin each line as slowly as possible and then with increasing speed read and read—breathlessly in mind only—until you reach the end of the line or sentence. What is it like to read this way? This eye-and-mind act turns into a game: *Can I get to the end of the poem before the next bout of clear-air turbulence?*

If you are an anxious flier, make your peace with writing as well as reading poems. Comfort yourself with the idea that nothing bad will happen in-flight while you are writing in the middle of a line … and yet don't linger there for fear that you won't get to the end of your poem if something catastrophic does happen. The thought is paradoxical and preposterous, but that doesn't change the fact that the act of writing a poem on a plane can feel powerful. At times the writing feels like a diversion from flying, at other times it feels like an animation of the experience. Once in a while it may feel like a bit of both—like that threshold between being asleep and being awake, where for a moment you lose all sense of where and even who you are. Writing a poem in flight: this is checking out at its most sublime, and it allows for an equanimity you will simply never achieve on the ground.

Writing

There are so many things one could do other than write poems. Take a long walk. Examine a beautiful tree for disease. Pick up a rock; throw it into a lake or at a passing car. Pick a flower; tape it to that rock and drop it from the edge of a canyon. Do this over and over until a small part of the canyon is filled. For writing poems often feels as though it amounts to as much: arranging a pile of stones for someone else to haul elsewhere.

A poet may argue that poetry and life interact in such a way that makes life more poetic, or that a certain kind of life drives and inspires poem-making. Either case belies the reason someone writes poems: it is simply something to do.

Writing poetry is an act of cleaving—attracting you to and separating you from others at the same time. So ask yourself: What is it that you hope to get from writing poems? Sophistication? Empathy? A career path? Laid?

The reward is not that the poems will be rewarded. The reward is intrinsic in the highs and lows of writing them, where the external reward may only be to take a break, to go for that walk, or to mind the precipices along the canyon.

First Principles

A poem is a made thing: the product of a process that involves writing and reading and rewriting.

Writing a poem is not a preplanned act, but an act of discovery. It's nearly impossible, for instance, to write a memorable poem for one's mother on Mother's Day. Having a top-down idea like that will almost always stifle any ideas other than received ones. Let a poem grow from the bottom up. Instead of "I have an idea for a poem about a squirrel who's trapped in a tree," write some squirrely lines and see where they take you. The process should be one of poetic as well as personal adventure.

Written language, especially poetry, is inherently a flawed translation of lived life. This sentence included.

The sooner you admit that poems are trivial, the sooner you can grow to appreciate life for treating you so trivially.

If writing attempts to make something that is not the case appear true, living attempts to make writing about it appear falser than it is. All the striving of writing poetry is also a striving to transcend poetry.

A poet begins each poem hoping it will be the greatest poem of all time—not because she wants fame, but because she wants to not have to write poems anymore.

Life doesn't sentence us; we sentence life.

I love you. For the sentiment to hold meaning, view each word as an actor helping to put on a small show for an audience of one.

As a poet, you get to tell your own origin story. In the beginning there was a word...then another word...and before long there was an epigram, a proverb, a parable, a commandment, a *pensée*, a koan, and an epitaph. For once upon a time poetry was lyrical and satirical. Aphorisms were epic. (Ordinary prose was poetic.) And epics were pieced together with epithets—mnemonic phrases linking character and setting and plot...Homer's infamous "wine-dark" sea and "rosy-fingered" dawn.... Then there came the jokes. Joyce's "snotgreen sea," "scrotumtightening sea." And "wine-dark" turned out to be a (mis)translation that still flummoxes scholars: *Should it be "wine-like," "wine-ish," "wine-faced"? Did the Greeks maybe drink blue wine?* For, in retrospect, there was a lot of mistranslation.

All writing is creative writing, or none of it is.

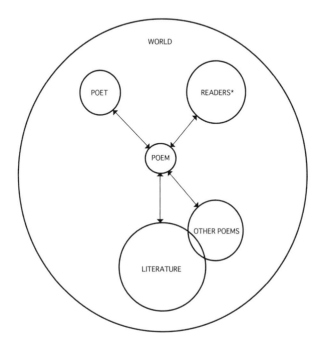

* 50% OTHER POETS; 10% FAMILY; 10% FRIENDS, 10% STUDENTS; 10% (EX-)LOVERS; 10% UNKNOWN

(FIGURES APPROXIMATE)

Form

Form is codified practice. Ceremonial, ritual—as in Latin *ritus* or Sanskrit *ṛtá*: a proven way of doing something, an order.

Young poets often believe that conventional forms are too restrictive. They don't want to live by other people's rules. *All these others went before me and this is as good as it gets?* One can understand the frustration.

The case against conventional forms is easy to make: the ineffable, say, view of the Grand Canyon from a scenic outlook, doesn't speak to us in strict rhyme or meter. And yet there's still the presence of language—that sign "Scenic Overlook" that indicated the best spot for us to capture the moment.

Poetry's "rules" are not meant to be obeyed blindly; they are to be employed. That is, parameters don't hinder but aid in composition. *How long should this line be? How long should this poem be?* If you chose a conventional form, even something as simple as the same number of syllables per line, you have enough limitations to focus your attention. If you chose a sonnet, for example, you know that you don't have to write more than fourteen lines, that the last two should couple up, and that your subject matter is love or unrequited love.

There's little reason to shun the sonnet, villanelle, ghazal, pantoum, or to avoid structures such as terza rima, heroic couplets, and blank verse. They lie there like blueprints in a cabinet you've never used before. Take one out and figure out what it's for, what it does.

The architect Louis Sullivan gave us the concept *form follows function*; the purpose of a building should guide how it's designed and constructed. Sullivan's mentee Frank Lloyd Wright modified the concept: *form and function are one*. This sounds a lot like Alexander Pope: *The sound must seem an echo to the sense*. Beyond a generic idea of communication, what's the function of your poem?

Form frees you from the patterns you already have. Resistance to form is resistance to changing your own habits, good or bad.

If you want to write in form, begin with the haiku and tanka, or the acrostic and telestich—all easy-to-learn structures that can lead to more complex ones.

Form follows precedent. If one traditional form doesn't inspire, try the multitude of others: ode, fable, bestiary, fabliau, riddle, rondeau, hymn, ballad, gospel, panegyric, ghazal, pantoum, abecedarian, etc.

Form incarnates itself multifariously. Borrow the forms of other kinds of writing: letter, law brief, lab report, executive summary, personal ad, portrait, still life, memo, errata, recipe, to-do list, instruction manual—or any other quotidian or ephemeral text you can think of.

Form is a template to be modified.

Sonnet

Allegedly invented by a Sicilian lawyer, popularized by Petrarch and Dante, fortified by Herbert, Donne, and Shakespeare, practiced by Milton, Shelley, Wordsworth, Hopkins, Rossetti, and innumerable others on its way to the twentieth century, the sonnet is a form that never seems to go out of style. Notable contemporary variations include:

- Ted Berrigan's "shared sonnets" that rely on the repeated cutting and pasting of the same lines (often from other poets) to illustrate that with the form, with love, and with time "Whatever is going to happen is already happening."

- Olena Kalytiak Davis' "shattered sonnets" that document wounded love and its vestiges by pounding the form with sound until the form "shatters" into sixteen lines.

- Jen Bervin's "Nets" that "strip Shakespeare's sonnets bare to the 'nets'" and on the page look something like lineated cobwebs with black word-flies caught in them.

Keeping as many parameters as you can—a rhyme scheme, a turn (volta), a closing couplet—write a sonnet in a single sentence (cf. Robert Frost's "The Silken Tent") or a sonnet of fourteen words, one word per line. Or make up your own variation, Sonneteer.

```
P   E   N   P   A   P   E   R
O   C   C   A   S   I   O   N   A   L
T       E       A       R       S
Y   O   U   R   T   R   A   G   I   C
H           O           P           E
T   O   B   E   C   O   M   E
A   B   E   L   O   V   E   D
P           O           E           T
S   H   O   U   L   D   N   O   T
H           A           N           G
O           N           A           N
E   P   I   G   R   A   M

C   A   L   L   M   O   M
A   N   D   D   A   D


S   O   N   N   E   T
```

Self-Expression

Nearly all young poets begin writing in order to express themselves. This is fine as far as it goes, but far too many overlook the possibility of expressing the world.

Keeping a secret journal or diary is the purest form of self-expression. Your dreams and fears can spill out, formed or unformed, without the surveillance, promotion, or accomplice of social media. A journal also provides a record for your future self—a body of work that can be mined for poems at a later time when you can reflect on your experience.

The idea of "finding your voice" is more of a hindrance than an aid. As a poet, there is no reason to keep to one voice. No matter what you do—even in trying the most random of writing exercises—you will not able to escape your voice.

Any poem that has a first person speaker is actually a persona poem. But do not worry, as Pessoa says, "To pretend is to know oneself."

Which of the following best describes you?

A) Go-getter.

B) Soul-searcher.

C) Bad boy/bad girl.

D) Cute.

E) Old enough not to give a shit about the question.

When you realize that you contain multitudes, try not to be too disappointed.

Using "i" in a poem confers less humility than using the conventional "I." That is, "i" draws more, not less, attention to itself. It is a naive gesture, and is allowed exclusively in the work of e e cummings, who only agreed to the use of no caps in his name at the urging of his publisher.

T. S. Eliot argued that the schizophrenic's point of view is not only valid but must be appreciated. This is not exactly what Rimbaud meant when he wrote *Je est un autre*: I is an other. But if you too believe in your Self and your Other, remember that it's difficult to get both to speak at once.

You might know who you are, but do you know *what* you are? Sit on your hands until they fall asleep and no longer feel like a part of you. (Bite them a little to make sure.) Then look around at all the objects in the room. Books and chairs and colorful rectangles on the walls. The walls themselves—what are they to you? And you to them? Begin typing.

You are a construct. And this fact will become most clear when you sit at your father's deathbed as he's dying of rectal cancer, and have to sum up his life for him. There is little more inscrutable than writing a eulogy over the course of several weeks or months that begins to take on the qualities of a novel, and must be pared down to a few paragraphs which should sound nothing like a prose poem. The act of the eulogy will make writing the obituary easier, like writing the caption to photo that exists only for your father's funeral. If you have any doubts about your being a construct, they will be answered on your own deathbed.

You strike through the mask—Melville's term for the veil of ineffability—by wearing a mask. In other words: you don't find your voice, you make it.

Over time, authenticity may begin to feel simply like an opinion. As when looking at a painting in a museum, the most authentic part about it may well be the nail on which it hangs.

Sometimes it takes more courage to clothe, not bare, your soul.

Writing doesn't compete with reality so much as it completes it. You will never know the exact end of the story of your life, but there's no harm in imagining and writing your own obituary— many times over. Your identity is based on your memories and your memories are based on your imagination.

How do I know what I feel until I see how badly I write, wrote Anonymous.

Try writing a series of personal poems without using "I." It may or may not help to remember that even Narcissus couldn't see his reflection in running water.

"For years I railed against being put in this category [Confessionalism]," said Anne Sexton, "then … I decided I was the only confessional poet." Ultimately, the category we put Sexton into doesn't matter. We can argue that Sexton expressed "her self" in her poems, but it's more valuable to understand that she expressed what women were not supposed to express at the time—subjects like menstruation, abortion, sex, addiction, and suicide.

If the self involves multiple selves, or at least multiple roles, then the way to get at self-expression is to play out as many as you can. One line of reasoning goes that the more characters or points of view you can write from, the more complete, the more objective your own story. Or perhaps that misses point. If you come at something from enough perspectives, you may lose all perspective. Perhaps missing the point is the point.

Sublimation

If you can't love the one you want to in real life, then you find a healthy alternative: you sublimate that love into art. Instead of making love, in other words, you make a poem.

The idea is that you put your loss into the page and it becomes a kind of gain: a few lines, maybe a poem, conceivably a book. But the written words actually trace a new loss, a literal marking of the maker's time on the page. If the work survives to publication, the lines will rise momentarily when someone else reads them, only for the purpose of being lost again.

Elizabeth Bishop's "One Art" is seemingly about loss—all the repeated losses one has to or will experience in life—from house keys to loved ones. The last lines go like this:

> … It's evident
> the art of losing's not too hard to master
> though it may look like (*Write* it!) like disaster.

The final line—specifically, what's between those parentheses—is crucial to a certain understanding of the poem. The poem is no longer about loss and disaster, it's about *writing* about loss and disaster; they are not the same thing. The speaker at the end of "One Art" is writing about loss—the loss of the "you"—in order to make the loss at once more authentic *and* more artful, legitimate, and purged.

A poet writes a love poem for his beloved, but it's not really an expression of love for his beloved. It's an expression of love for himself. Sublimation: A martyr rushes into a phone booth, makes a small fuss, and then bursts out Mr. Arty.

"No artist tolerates reality," wrote Nietzsche. The very fact of writing a poem bears out the idea: art is both unreal and real at the same time. The clearest example is the stage play where there are two simultaneous realities: the reality of what's happening on stage between characters and the reality of the audience sitting and watching the first reality. In other words, to be alive is always to be between the imaginary and the real, and your reading this sentence is just enough proof.

Sublimation is supposed to be cathartic. But it can feel that with every word you write another piece of your life is being destroyed.

If you experience a terrible event, you will slowly dilute it by writing about it. But if you don't write about it, it will slowly dilute you. What you realize sooner or later is that you can no more rewrite wrongs than you can rewrite rights.

Imitation

"Anxiety of influence"—the idea that reading others' work will inhibit your own—is a myth. Cultivate influence. Poetry, as with all arts, is generative. One work builds on another, or one work attempts to un-build another (in both cases, the more recent work is still generative). The premise of Harold Bloom's eponymous essay is that great poets respond to other great poets because they are trying to imitate them. But the act of imitation is never fully possible—mostly because of *misreading*, not inability—and what results is the making of new, great poems.

For a contemporary poet or reader, the key point of T. S. Eliot's essay "Tradition and the Individual Talent" is that a new work that implies, references, or invokes an old work necessarily modifies the old work. This means that even, say, watching a movie like *Shakespeare in Love* may change the way you see *Romeo and Juliet*—even if you don't want it to.

Furthermore, the order in which you view or read a work also shapes how you understand works as they relate to each other. Seeing *Shakespeare in Love* or *West Side Story* before you read *Romeo and Juliet* or any of Shakespeare's sonnets will inform, for better or worse, your readings of the original work—the original work in fact may not seem as original simply because it has come to you as a kind of "copy," in a second or a third position.

Shakespeare's Dog

To imitate or not to imitate? There really is no question. Imitation is how you've learned to do things ever since you were a child. It is the route into and out of yourself.

Imitation involves close reading. Take the beginning of Wallace Stevens' "Thirteen Ways of Looking at a Blackbird":

I.
Among twenty snowy mountains,
The only moving thing
Was the eye of the blackbird.

II.
I was of three minds …

Did you read the section headings "I." and "II." aloud? If so, you might have realized that "I." also seems like the first-person "I" for a moment, or that "II." (as in "two") sounds for a moment like it connects with "three" in the following line. And did you consider that the "three minds" in the second stanza might refer back to the first stanza's "mountains," "eye," and "blackbird"? Maybe all that sounds like a reach, but if you continue examining the poem you'll find a pattern of such playfulness. The point: if you want to imitate "Thirteen Ways," focus on the juxtapositions and transitions of the poem, not simply on its many "ways of looking."

Imitation is exceedingly difficult, sometimes boring, and utterly necessary. There's nothing wrong with the enterprise as long as you keep a good amount of aspirin on hand. It's important to bring your idols down from on high; try referring to them by nickname. Don't call the Son of God, Jesus or Christ, call him Jeez or Jessie. Not Mohammed, but Mo. Not Mother Teresa, but Terry. Yes, irreverence has its place in worship. Remember that the great books lay their grace chiefly between your hands.

Whatever is new to you is old to someone else. There's no shame or insecurity in it. *Writing has always been hard.* Tattoo it on the back of your hand or frame it over your desk. To be honest, there's no such thing as writing; there's only re-writing.

Try not to worry about originality so much. Because you didn't invent the language you speak or write, you will never be completely original. (Moses, after all, plagiarized most of the Commandments.)

Ezra Pound's admonition to "make it new" is, essentially, a mistranslation. He lifted it from an inscription on an ancient Chinese daily washing bowl that read "do it again," as in don't forget to wash behind your ears every day. Both the original and the translation are important. "Do it again" might well mean "keep at it," which if taken to heart, might result in something new.

Don't try. That's the epitaph on Charles Bukowski's gravestone. Does it mean "don't bother to try because you're going to fail anyway"? Does it mean "don't *just* try, do it, keep at it until you succeed"? Or does it mean "don't try too hard ... *let* it come to you, let it happen"? All are possibilities, even all at once. It's also a corollary to Pound's "make it new": the idea that it would be so easy just to say it's all been done before.

Avant-Garde

An elderly painter once said that the definition of the avant-garde is simply the people with the most energy. The same is true of poetry.

We may be inclined to always put experimental poetry in quotes. What's "experimental" today may either become conventional or simply forgotten tomorrow. More often than not, an "experimental" poem is one that wants to be treated as an unidentifiable object first, a piece of communication second. Something someone can point to and say, *Look at this wondrous/ strange/mystical thing!*

Dickinson and Stein. Their work is still as avant-garde, as challenging as anything today in U.S. poetry. If you want to venture further, the sourcebook for experimental poems to read and/or use as jumping off points is the two-volume *Poems for the Millennium* edited by Jerome Rothenberg and Pierre Joris, whose commentaries on poets, poetries, and movements are as thought-provokingly experimental as the poems themselves.

Songs with poetic lyrics—from folk and rock to pop and hip-hop—not only replaced patterned rhymed and rhythmed poetry in the twentieth century, they improved on it. *Poets, you are free*, musicians said, *to do other things!* And so some poets invented anti-musical poems, anti-imagistic poems, and simply anti-poems.

L=A=N=G=U=A=G=E poetry, or just Language poetry when the poets who write it are feeling less ill at ease, engages in disjunctive syntax in an effort to subvert political and social norms. If manipulating language has power ("the word made flesh"), then up-ending its rules entirely would seem like a good idea. But the high level of arbitrariness in Language poetry usually just ends up isolating the poets who write it.

Typically, a Language poem comes off as some kind of militaristic engagement (situation normal all fucked up) or as if the dictionary has upchucked on the page. You feel that if you lined up any number of Language poems in the world, at any particular moment, you really wouldn't be able to tell where one ended and the next began. This would appear to be somehow "freeing" if it weren't so artificial, or worse unmemorable. But Language poetry isn't about being memorable; it's about experiencing language's artificiality and using it to expose language's biases.

Lyn Hejinian, one of the founders of Language poetry, once wrote a book called *My Life*. It contains thirty-eight prose poems, each of which is thirty-eight sentences long. Some years later she published another edition of *My Life*, adding more poems and more sentences to correspond to her age. Hejinian has argued that the poems present an "open text," a story that never ends and that can never completely be told, one that resists narrative, resists order, etc. But the lovely prose poems of *My Life* are filled with echoing images and connective concepts, and they adhere to a system of their own rules (same number of stanzas, same number of sentences, each poem employing a provocative subtitle). The book tells a story much in the way a series of portraits do. In other words, once you find the patterns, *My Life* turns out to be pretty conventional.

Avant-garde forms tend to follow William Blake's admonition: Make your own system or be imprisoned by another's. Here are just five stand-out examples of innovative systems: Jean Toomer's *Cane*, an incomparable book that combines folk and elite, rural and urban, and black and white in poems, vignettes, dialogues, and brief narratives; Marianne Moore's compositional system of syllabics in poems such as "The Fish," "The Steeple-Jack," and "Black Earth"; John Berryman's *Dream Songs*, in which voices, registers, and vernacular are smashed together in poems of three, six-line irregularly rhymed stanzas; Christian Bök's *Eunoia*, a set of lipogrammatic "chapters," each containing only words that use one of the five vowels; Katie Degentesh's *The Anger Scale*, a book of Google-sculpted seriocomic poems based on the Minnesota Multiphasic Personality Inventory, the "gold standard in personality testing."

If you want to write an experimental poem that employs arbitrariness of line, phrase, or word juxtaposition, so be it. But have a good reason for each instance of arbitrariness—namely, that any other arbitrariness just wouldn't seem right.

While change can be a good thing in your work, you may not have to make an effort to affect it if you write long enough. Life continually changes around you. So if you don't change, you will still change because all else does. The issue becomes not whether change is good or bad, but in selecting which of the seemingly unchangeable things you still want to carry with you into the everything else that's always changing.

Art survives the art of it as abstraction survives the abstraction of it. What *it* is nobody really knows, but the avant-garde still hopes to know—exists to hope—even if it's been proven, with respect to every conceivable adverb, that hope has lied about where it came from.

Translation

The best way to understand your language is to get outside of it; that is, by learning another language. And the best way to learn another language is to immerse yourself in it—by living abroad. For a poet, there's no substitute for exile even if it must be self-imposed.

There's a whole world of poetry most of us ignore: foreign works in translation. Some say that you must read poems in their original language or not read them at all—that translations are always bastardizations. It seems like such a specious point when one begins to tally up all the extraordinary translations of the ancients all the way up to the twentieth-century luminaries like Anna Akhmatova, Constantine Cavafy, Marina Tsvetayeva, Federico García Lorca, and numerous others. And once you begin the endeavor, you find innumerable stunning works that have no English equivalents—from the poems of major figures like Adonis and Wisława Szymborska to those of the relatively unknown like Xi Chuan and Dunya Mikhail.

Ezra Pound put forth that he translated the poem "The River-Merchant's Wife: A Letter" from the original Chinese by Li Po when in fact Pound made most of it up. Instead of dismissing him as a con artist, though he played that role fabulously in other realms, one can take this poem as a fine starting point for poetry in translation in the twentieth century.

Either all translations of poems are invented, or poetry in translation is not possible and one must read poetry only in its original language. Pound's greatest legacy was his translation mistakes and hijinks, clearing a path for others like Robert Bly who began translating great stacks of poetry by Rilke, Ponge, Neruda, Vallejo, Rumi, Hafez, Kabir, Tranströmer, etc., with what appears to be just a set of bilingual dictionaries. That sounds harsh, but Bly's important work tilled an entire field for others to keep translations of non-English poems thriving.

A translation of a poem is itself an original poem. There are, therefore, two original poems: the original and the original that is called a translation.

Poetry in translation is, by definition, conceptual poetry.

Mistranslation begets wondrous things. For scholars have long determined that the proverb "It's easier for a fat man to pass through the eye of a needle than a rich man to enter the kingdom of heaven" is a mistranslation—the "fat man" should actually be a "thick cord of rope," which one has to admit could be forced through that eye with a lot of persistence.

Homophonic translation. Take a poem in a language you have absolutely no experience with but one that still has an alphabet you somewhat recognize—Swedish, Hungarian, Romansh, Middle English (*Sir Gawain and the Green Knight* works well). Without the help of a dictionary or digital translation, translate the poem by intuiting or imagining what the foreign words sound or look like in English. Make sure to look for repetitions and patterns. Homophonic work helps rejuvenate your aural/oral skills, especially if you want to work on sonics but are tired of trying to write in patterned rhyme from scratch.

Technique

A poetic style is something to cling to until it's outgrown. Some styles, like bad seeds, never grow.

Play your strengths. If you are good at writing dialogue, write poems all in dialogue. If you are good at writing in character, write persona poems. If you are good at plot, write short stories or a novel.

Certain quarters will admonish you to create a singular style—something to be "known" for. This would appear to be something to strive for. But to be wedded to one style prevents you from one of your foremost missions: linguistic promiscuity.

Fragmented poetry often purports to subvert the "normal" ways of daily discourse, worldview, or societal interaction, but as often it forgets that one's thoughts from moment to moment are fragmented. Thus, fragmented poetry becomes more mimetic and closer to verisimilitude than so-called conventional poetry.

The need or desire for fragmentation in poetry is a need or desire for putting your life into another order—or to flesh out the notion that all order is ostensible.

The world wants order, and so does your poetry. Free verse is no freer than the right angles at the corners of the page that box in your poem. In a free verse poem, as in an abstract painting, the choices are terrifying and seemingly endless.

Take one of your free verse poems. Scan the lines to see and hear what can be taken advantage of rhythmically. Iambic lines at the end of a poem can indicate closure. A weak ending (an unstressed syllable) can indicate uncertainty or melancholy as music does in a minor key. But it all depends. None of this takes into account the pitch of your voice as you read the words aloud.

Skim texts (including your own poems) so that you misread lines. Misreadings are invaluable building blocks. So are mishearings; mondegreen your way, for example, through REM's 1983 album *Murmur*. And don't forget to learn from and to mine your typos.

Don't fall into the trap of viewing found poetry as lesser than "original" poetry. To make her artwork, a sculptor either takes a material, such as clay, and builds it up, or takes a large piece of material, such as marble, and carves out the artwork. The latter method is the method of found poetry: it is made from linguistic marble—already existing printed, digital, or otherwise written down texts, including novels, manuals, newspaper articles, grocery lists, letters, advertisements, and captions. The original text(s) may be excerpted, cropped or shimmied, blackened or whited out, or variously manipulated to create a different, "new" text. Found poetry has a long tradition that includes the pastiche ("cut-up") and the cento, a conventional form in which you compose a hundred-line poem by taking one line from a hundred different poems.

The notion that to break a rule one must know the rules first expresses a desire to have no rules. If one does not like a rule, say, rhymed couplets or blank verse, it is not because there is a flaw in the rule, but because one wasn't the first to invent it.

If you want to make a statement or put forward a "truth," try doing it from a character's mouth. Poetry readers are more inclined to buy what even an "unlikeable" character says in dialogue than what an "unlikeable" first person speaker says forthrightly. In a novel, we grant "unreliable" narrators a good deal of leeway; however, in lyric poetry, we prefer our speakers to be purer than fiction.

Refrain from using the phrase "stream of consciousness" to describe a poem's movement or thought processes. Every poem is a stream of consciousness, some more, some less organized. More importantly, to generalize that a poem's loose associations are stream of consciousness is to make judgments about how thinking is supposed to happen.

Anticipate reader's expectations: what some poets call "surprise." Foiling or playing off expectations can mean writing the opposite of what a reader might expect—but even oppositions can become expected, clichéd. Consider all or other possibilities for your oppositions. What is, for example, the opposite of an orange? An apple? A fig? A snowball? A tricycle? A scream?

Adjectives are almost always the last, not the first, thing to think about when making a poem. The juxtaposition of nouns is far more important than the adjectives that may be on hand to modify them.

Much discussion is made about poetry meant for the page versus poetry meant for the stage (spoken word). For the most part, discover the differences yourself by composing what you think is one and then the other. There are strengths and weaknesses to both. The page allows for graphic effects (cf. page as canvas) and visual line break effects that can't be heard aloud. The performance of a poem is just that—a performance. If done well, spoken word uses vocal pitch, tone, and dynamics—along with perhaps some shtick—that can't be conveyed by any other means than acting.

When you deliver spoken word poems, remember that silences, as well as sounds, produce notes. And do not fear the stage: the audience doesn't know what it wants until you tell them what it wants.

If you want models for persona poems, you can examine Robert Browning's "My Last Duchess" or T. S. Eliot's "The Love Song of J. Alfred Prufrock" or the poems of Ai's *Vice*. Or, you can do what young actors do: study the monologues of plays.

"First words, best words" is okay advice if you are going to go back and edit all those first words to make them the best of the best.

Ginsberg said that a line's length should be equal to a breath. This may be helpful in your shaping of phrases or lines, but remember that everyone breathes at different rhythms and at increased or decreased rates in certain situations (sex, exercise, coma). Breath is no absolute guide for the line.

Charles Olson talked about breath-centric poems or poems being OPEN FIELDS. In his Projective Verse manifesto, he writes, "ONE PERCEPTION MUST IMMEDIATELY AND

DIRECTLY LEAD TO A FURTHER PERCEPTION." And he quotes Robert Creeley, "FORM IS NEVER MORE THAN AN EXTENSION OF CONTENT." In practical terms, this seems to point to a foregrounding or displaying of the process of writing over its product, or the process as the product. We might be back to Ginsberg's "first words, best words," or André Breton's automatic writing that, as its best practitioners know, must be edited later so that it appears more automatic.

The breath you should really worry about is the one you hear yourself take before a line is read aloud. This is particularly audible on live radio where you can hear every little inhalation the speaker takes. Paying attention to your breath as you read aloud is probably the most visceral way of connecting to the one who created the work.

If you think you are recording memories in a poem, think again: they are not memories; they are recreations you want to recall in the future.

A poem can be as much about forgetting as it is about remembering.

Do not fill your poems with generalizations that aim to be "universal." The imagination comes to universality through details and idiosyncracies. A detail is never a bad place to begin a poem; it is the bait on the hook of your line.

Emily Dickinson is allowed to leave her poems untitled. For every other poet, the lack of a title is either a missed opportunity or an admission that the poet himself doesn't care enough about the poem for anyone to bother with it.

Don't put the word "dream" in the title of a poem. A poem is already a kind of dream.

Synesthesia is copacetic to use in a poem, but don't tell others that you perceive the number seven as blue or that when you hear middle C you taste cherry tomatoes. It's just going to embarrass you and make them feel inferior.

Forego the idea of jotting down lines in your phone. Buy a pen and a pocket notebook. Find a notebook that is an odd shape: a square or an old journalist's long pad. Or cut paper into long strips and carry them around in your pockets. Even if you don't use them, they will make you feel a certain degree of guilt, which is a fine place to begin writing.

Italics can add another layer to a poem: italicized words or phrases form a subset, a poem within a poem. But do not rely on italics to emphasize a word or a phrase; rely on the perspicacity of the word or phrase itself, or on repetition.

Make time and space for unstructured play—not only when you first begin writing a poem, but throughout all its drafts. Whenever you get stuck, take any book down from the shelf. Before opening, ask it a random question such as: What's for dinner? Who invented Christmas caroling? Why won't my son brush his teeth before bed? How long before I die? Then open the book, point without looking, and read your answer.

If you worry too much about whether your readers will be offended by what you write, take up something that's still beneficent to others but less problematic, like pyrotechnics or beekeeping.

The Creative Writing Classroom

The creative writing classroom is both a workshop and a staging area. On the one hand, it is an informal, garage-style site for making and taking apart texts. On the other, it is a time and space to display and consider a selection of made objects in a more formal way.

In the workshop, the teacher can't tell the student how to write a poem. But the teacher can help the student get his or her mind into a state of play; play is where poems come from. Learning how to write poems becomes less about knowledge acquisition and more about behavior modification. For example, as an assignment, request that students brush their teeth with their nondominant hands the night before the next class. Their reports back about the experience will run like this: "It was hard and awkward." "It was like doing it for the first time." "It took me longer than usual." "I had to think about it a lot." Thinking along these lines is exactly the mind-set you want them in when writing a poem.

A writing workshop should really be called a writing *and* reading workshop, or a language laboratory. There is no end to the work-shop type endeavors you and your students can pursue—from imitating conventional structures and forms to trying out Dadaist and Surrealist games or any of Bernadette Mayer's writing experiments (all easily found online). Make sure to dedicate specific class meetings for research trips (library, field), collaboration, and revision.

With so much play going on, it may occur to you that the classroom is like a little black box theater. The students are the actors. The teacher is the director/actor. The poems students write are their costumes, masks. Every speech-act is largely scripted. The protagonist is whoever is talking. The supporting cast includes whoever is listening. However, the little black box is a failure of design: it lacks a real audience .... Skip the analogy, find an actual black box theater or a performance stage, make the actors memorize each other's lines, see if they've written anything worth producing.

For God's sake keep the classroom door closed. Either the teacher's or the students' feng shui energy will leak out, or other students and colleagues will listen in on the class's unorthodox methods.

The Workshop

The teacher should lead a mock workshop (a practice run) using a poem none of the workshop members has written— something the teacher has drafted up, a previous student's draft, or even a published poem that seems unfinished. Examine and discuss the poem and solicit suggestions for possible improvements. Then, project it on a large screen or monitor and for thirty minutes and in silence let them watch you cut, add, re-cut, stare, mumble, struggle—based on the workshop's suggestions as well as your own. Let them witness the sheer tedium of revision. Then, have a volunteer do the same in front of the class for another thirty minutes. In the next class meeting compare the original version, your version, and the student's version.

There are various ways in which to run an actual workshop. You can workshop poems cold, so to speak, those that the students have just brought in to class; or, you can workshop poems that have been distributed days or a week in advance so that everyone has prepared comments. In either case, before a poem is to be critiqued, hear it aloud twice. First, have it read by a peer and then by the poet. The other readers should listen for differences in the two readings, and the poet should listen for places that her peer stumbles.

The writing workshop critique is somewhat like a studio art critique: a piece is set in front of others for comprehension, inspection, and advice-giving. Unfortunately, too many of these critiques begin "I like it/I don't like it." One's initial admiration or distaste for a poem is a valid but usually unhelpful response. Go ahead and have that first impression, just make sure that a workshop critique doesn't become a popularity contest.

There is nothing wrong with some feel-good, warm-fuzzy comments at the beginning of a critique. These are often made as initial concessions to get the poet to be receptive; once dispensed, the real critique may begin.

Reiterating Alexander Pope's *An Essay on Criticism*, Samuel Coleridge reminds us to use "genial criticism." Let us make suggestions about the poem being workshopped in an effort to make it the best "of its kind." This means beginning from what the poem intends, not what we may intend for the poem. For example, if I detest squirrels, having lost the tip of my index finger to one as a toddler, and the poem before me is about squirrels, I can't help but have an immediate and adverse response to the poem. But however long it takes (a minute, an hour, a day) I should set aside my aversion and proceed: If this poem is going to be about squirrels, how can I help it to be the best damn squirrel poem ever?

If you are the poet whose work is getting critiqued, learn how to interpret the nonverbal communication of your teacher and peers. There are macroexpressions such as crossed arms, leaning forward or back, rolling eyes, and sleeping; and, there are microexpressions such as nose wrinkling, narrowing of the lips, and rising eyebrows. Microexpressions are crucial in determining what people really think of your poems (in case they are not forthright in their comments) as well as for accustoming yourself to the subtleties of poems themselves.

The author of a poem is the poem's first reader. The author is also the poem's last reader, because once the poem is read by someone else it becomes another poem.

Workshop comment: "I think this line was intentional because … ." Cut this kind of thing off. *Everything* is intentional: it's all on the page, right? If it weren't intentional, you wouldn't be looking at it.

Resist using the word "flow" to talk about how a poem moves or sounds—"I really like the flow of this" or "this flows well"—it's vague b.s. Unless you want to get specific, with the use of a flow diagram as a rapper might, the best thing one can say about flow is that it's *wolf* spelled backwards.

Workshop comment: "That poem is so *honest.*" Really? It's not honest; it's artifice. Or, is the idea that it's *true*? But what isn't true? True to one's own experience, or the experience of the poem? Be careful of using terminology that sets up false demarcations—Honesty and Truth over here, and trickery and comedy over there—or that creates a hierarchy in which earnestness is inherently of a higher order than comedy. More often than not it's the interplay between registers, specifically tragicomedy, that cuts us to the pith, that allows us to endure the unendurable.

Avoid the word "creative" in describing a poem or a poet. Creative is shorthand for "I like it" which is shorthand for something you are attracted to but are too lazy to detail adequately.

The word "honest" in describing a poem is as useful as a mop is to a dentist.

The workshop teacher is an authority who must fake being an authority. If what a student wants from the workshop teacher is his or her overt and glowing praise (or at least approval), the student will be disappointed—not because the teacher is not willing to offer such, but because every work put forward in a workshop is a draft that exists to be "improved."

The real products of empathy in a workshop are not the poems written for it, but the in-class experiences themselves—the chaotic interaction of ideals and ideas and the observations of members' frailties. If a workshop turns into group hug therapy, relish it. Outside of class, poetry is, intrinsically, a lonely pursuit.

Next time you are in a workshop take a good look around. Who in the room reminds you most of yourself? Is it the same person who gives you the most critical feedback? The one whose poems are most like yours? Who in the room is your "opposite"? What are your criteria for making such a choice? Out of a workshop of, say, ten to fifteen, home in on the two or three peers whose comments are the least useful to you. Is the problem with them or with you?

It's easy to dismiss workshop member comments that don't seem useful to you. But suppose they are the only people who are going to buy your future book—how are you going get them to turn the pages?

Advice from other readers and poets will often appear redundant—that is, you will be told to make the same or very similar changes to your poems. But this is not "majority rules," or remotely a democratic process. Writing, especially rewriting, is often a draconian endeavor.

Before your next workshop, consider this: 80 percent of your peers won't be writing poems a year after they graduate and 95 percent of them won't be writing poems five years from now. On the one hand, this fact is meant to motivate you to work harder— to be one of the chosen by choosing yourself. On the other hand, the same percentages could hold true for your classmates in math, science, or history courses.

Peer Review

Intent. Your first job is to discern the poem's intent or "overall picture." Begin broadly: Is it a song, a narrative, a scene, a monologue, a fragment, etc.? Then sharpen focus: Is the poem trying to recast an old myth, lament about a past event, meditate on a banality, etc.? Consider structure: Does the poem use a recognizable structure or traditional form? Is it riffing on other forms—love letter, manifesto, rant, deposition, portrait, op-ed piece, instruction manual, etc.? Keep in mind that the poem's intent may be various and combinatorial.

Examination. Indicate specific phrases, lines, patterns that point to the poem's intent(s); that is, provide evidence for your claims. (Look for places where the poem may even be telling you how to read it: "meta" moments.) Point out what is and what is not working toward the intent(s). Point out phrases and lines that are striking. Look for expected moments (cliché, received language), and instead of merely telling the poet to omit them, offer detailed suggestions about how to move toward unexpectedness. This may be as simple as switching out one word, or providing an "opposite" to the line at hand.

Further Examination. Run through your "cheat sheet" for inspecting specific patterns of word choice, rhythm, sound, imagery, idea, tone, line or stanza length, tense, point of view, character. These may be combined as needed. For example, examine closely the point(s) of view and the characters: Would the poem benefit from changing from first to second or third person, or exchanging the "I" and "you"? Would the poem be more interesting if genders were reversed? Are the characters specific characters (e.g., Judy, Marvin) or archetypal characters (e.g., father, girl), and what would happen if they were interchanged, made more specific or more anonymous?

Suggestions. For the next version(s) of the poem, offer *detailed* suggestions—not simply "add another stanza" or "change the point of view," but "tie the last stanza to the first with only one word," or "hold off naming the speaker's object of hatred until the speaker shows some hatred herself." This may involve scenario-making or "what-ifs": "What if the poem were told from the lover's sister's point of view in the past tense allowing the speaker more distance to reflect?" or "The second and tenth lines make a gorgeous couplet—what if you made a version all in couplets beginning with that one?"

Make at least one suggestion that is "radical," which may have to do with changing the poem's intent entirely.

Revision

Do not think of revision as correction; think of it as opening up the possibilities of what's already on the page.

Refrain from using the word *revision*, as it connotes that something is wrong, that something needs to be fixed. Use the word *version*, as in *I'm going to write three new versions of this poem.*

Is making new versions worthwhile? Whitman first published *Leaves of Grass* in 1855, and spent the rest of his life making new, and arguably many less successful versions. It seems he wanted the book to grow and age as he did, and so he kept editing and expanding it: six versions including the last "deathbed" edition.

Over the course of a half-century, Marianne Moore recapitulated her poem "Poetry" at least eleven times in publication. In 1919, she initially published the poem with thirteen lines. In 1935, when she included the poem in her *Selected Poems*, the poem had thirty-eight lines. And in 1967, in her *Complete Poems* she trimmed it down to three lines. "Poetry" is her most anthologized poem.

Continually reworking drafts, Elizabeth Bishop published only a hundred poems in her lifetime. She wrote "One Art," a villanelle that is so exquisite the form itself should be abandoned. But "The Moose" on which she worked for more than twenty years still has a title that gives too much away.

Work on one poem at a sitting. You most likely are distracted all day by all kinds of information. To concentrate on a single patch of words or lines for hours is not so much an act of singularity as it is of keeping everything else at bay.

Work on multiple poems at a sitting. You will invariably circle around the same preoccupations at any given moment, but you may need to come at your preoccupations from a variety of angles in order to do the deep diving.

Making new versions is a ton of work. Sitting around mulling over possible changes, speculating whether this or that small tweak or deletion might "help" the poem is a waste of time. You must actually do the work, trying a wide variety of options, often radical and resulting in failures, dozens of times over. So much so that someone looking at the initial version and the sixty-seventh (or whichever final version you settle on) will detect little if any resemblance between the two.

The best way to understand how structure and content inform each other isn't to read an essay or book about the topic. Instead, aim to find a paradigmatic (i.e., model) line length and a paradigmatic stanza. Try an arbitrary line length—any number of beats (2, 3, 5, etc.) or any number of syllables (5, 10, 15). Recompose each line using your parameter.

Try an arbitrary stanza length—couplets, triplets, quatrains, etc. The final version may not keep that structure, but in the process of refashioning the lines and stanzas, you will refashion the contents, too.

If you find a certain structure for your poems, keep writing in that structure until you find a way to make it collapse. Your destruction will become your improvement.

One of the most important structures of a poem is the same as for prose: the sentence. Put [ ] around each of the sentences in your poem. (If you've scorned punctuation, try putting it back in to see what the new version yields.) Right away you will notice short, long, medium sentences. Are they balanced or imbalanced? What's the effect of the long sentences, the short ones? What kind of effect would more variation or more regularization in sentence length have? Try breaking that long, gangly sentence into two or three sentences. Make a new version in which all the sentences are short, and another version of the poem that is one long sentence.

Some will tell you that you must take risks in your poems. These risks are probably not going to be what you think they are. They will not be, for the vast majority, writing willy-nilly all over the page, spurting out shock-n-cock lines about so-called taboo subjects, or scrawling down sins that are personal or confessional. What then are these risks? For most, they will be writing in regularized forms such as the sonnet, sestina, or in rhymed couplets. Where, after all, is the risk in doing what you want to do? Risk is about what you don't think you should be doing—challenging your own assumptions.

The point of a revision strategy is to find a way of re-engaging the poem. Possible strategies:

- Excise a successful stanza from a failed poem and a successful stanza from another failed poem; combine. Do this multiple times.

- Cut a poem in half, vertically. Take another poem and do the same. Splice together the differing halves.

- Write the opposite of every line in a version, which may yield a new poem entirely or just a line(s) that can be incorporated back into the initial version.

- Read aloud the last word of each line, which makes it a kind of subset or mini version of the poem. Do any words feel out of place? They aren't to be changed or deleted necessarily; they are to be inspected for their effects.

- Read aloud the first and last lines. What's the transformation between them? What kind of couplet do these lines make? Does it speak to the poem's intent? What happens if you exchange the lines?

- Modify a proofreading trick: Read the poem beginning with the last sentence, then the second to last, etc., all the way to the first sentence. Is it a better poem backwards?

- Shift the point of view of the poem—from "I" to "you" or "we" to "they" or "he" to "she." Try all combinations.

Notice that when you change "he" to "she," for
example, other connotations, gendered or not, begin
to change.

- Draw the scene, story, or impression of your poem. Then,
  without using a single word of your initial version, write
  a new poem based off of that drawing.

- Draw a flowchart of your poem, complete with boxes,
  shapes, and arrows. Now cut up all the elements and
  rearrange. Write a new version.

- Rewrite your poem from memory, with your
  nondominant hand.

As you are making versions the intent of the poem may often
change, repeatedly or radically, from the initial version. Let it.
This is the way toward poetical and personal discovery—what
Richard Hugo discusses variously in his collection of lectures
and essays *The Triggering Town*.

Perhaps the very best way to re-engage your work is to practice
separation anxiety (long-term peek-a-boo). Print out your
poems and mail them to a friend. Have the friend hold onto
them for six months and then mail them back. This process
might sound familiar: it's more or less how a poet used to submit
poems to a literary journal except that "a friend" was "an editor."

Similarly, you can put poems in a drawer for as long as it takes to remember that you've forgotten they were there (one, five, ten years; Horace recommended nine years). In the meantime, write other poems and put them in other drawers. There is no way to avoid that upon your death the drawers that still contain poems will be your best poems.

When do you stop making versions? Paul Valéry: *A poem is never finished, only abandoned.* It sounds plausible. But the question remains: When to abandon it? At the moment when doing any more to it—making new versions—only makes it worse? That usually simply indicates that you need a break from the poem—a poetic hiatus—and that you need to begin making new versions of some other half-abandoned poem.

Print out a few of your poems that you consider final versions (blown up to size 48 font), and tape them to a wall of your room, kitchen, office, etc. You need to see whether you can bear to look at, more or less live with, the poems in a tangible way. Also, affixing them to the wall allows you to make edits on the fly whenever you happen to notice the work. In the days or weeks or months that follow, the poems will show themselves as things of substance and lasting value—or they will not.

Poet-Teachers

A poet tries to become a teacher or professor in order to make a living. What he soon finds is that the salary is inadequate compensation, the grading induces migraines, and the administration continually seems to pose obstacles. He has probably anticipated most of this. But what he hasn't anticipated is the extent to which he never really understood poems (even if he has an MFA and a PhD) until he was made to teach them to others.

Many poets teach today not only out of a desire to make a living but out of a desire to have an audience. The audience, that is, for poems is primarily students, and the main stage for poems is the classroom. This is not as true in other arts—painting, music, dance, film—where the classroom is a stage to a greater stage— the gallery, the recital hall, the theater.

There are poet-teachers who are good instructors, and there are poet-teachers who are good entertainers. It is difficult to be both without compromising either.

The poet-teacher's job isn't only to impart knowledge; it is to question knowledge; it is to keep herself from being bored, or to invest herself fully in her boredom. The daily conundrum is to approach the poem(s) she is about to teach in class as if it's a long lost discovery. That means she shouldn't have an agenda for the poem(s). It means she shouldn't prep at all. It may even mean that class opens with her opening a book or poetry website at random and beginning where her finger or eye falls.

The poet-teacher should draw on the ways in which she survived other teachers, other guides—particularly those that presented her with obstacles.

Intentionally or not, poet-teachers try to convince their students to write like they do.

A good poet-teacher pushes the student on a path to make his or her own path. A good poet-teacher pushes the student to try things he or she doesn't want to.

A student can always learn something from a teacher who is older than him, simply because the teacher has more life experience, if not more reading and writing experience. The quality of that experience doesn't matter; it's only quantity that counts.

A student's best teachers won't chiefly be teachers—they will be poems themselves. The best thing any teacher can do, therefore, is to suggest specific poems and poets to the student that may help inform his or her work.

Vonnegut once remarked that long before creative writing teachers existed there were creative writing teachers—they were called editors. But now editors have almost all become gatekeepers to publication, and literary agents have become what editors used to be: creative writing teachers. Poets, however, don't have literary agents: they still need creative writing teachers.

How to grade creative writing? In a workshop course, this can pose difficulties for both teacher and student. There are a few options: give grades based on effort and the "risks" a student takes in his or her writing; effectively eliminate grades (everyone gets an "A" or a "P" for pass); or, have students give themselves their own grades. None of these is ideal. Perhaps the best thing to do is not to grade their creative works at all, but grade their written peer reviews exclusively. A student grade, then, is based on how well she or he critically examines others' work, particularly in suggestions for revision, in a formalized review (not only a few handwritten notes or oral comments in class).

In grading, the grand hope is that students will absorb a teacher's comments in detail and will enter into a dialogue with the teacher, in person or in writing. The reality is that the teacher marks the work just enough so as to justify the grade.

Professionalization

Although some lament the professionalization and academicization of poetry, let us not pretend that poetry has never had patrons. The college or university is a friend to the poet. In the classroom the poet is afforded a time and place to think and talk about what she wants to think and talk about—all before a ready-made audience.

Most universities have become corporations that prioritize revenue generation above all else, transforming the student into the customer-who-is-always-right. But what is a professor to do when a student gives a wrong answer? Like a poem, a professor can offer no money-back guarantee.

Tenured poets: the lucky, the guilty-ridden, the snickersneeing few.

In English Departments, you may now begin a sentence with "because," end a sentence with a preposition, or even find "homing in" indistinguishable from "honing in"—language adapts to its usage. But God help you if you mistake Frankenstein for his monster, mispronounce "Don Juan," or put an apostrophe on *Finnegans Wake*.

In academia much will be made of the length of your CV.

```
            G       E
        T   T   O       O
    C   L   O       S       E
A               N               D
I           '       L       L
S       P       L       I       T
Y       O       U       R
    I   N   F   I   N
        I       T       I
        V   E   S
```

```
A   C   A   D   E   M   I   C
F   R   E   E   D   O   M
```

Master of Fine Arts

If the greatest readership for poetry is other poets, then the thing to do is to turn more people into poets. At least that would seem as pragmatic as any premise for an MFA program.

To argue against the MFA system because it manufactures cookie-cutter poets and writers is crude, unobservant, and perhaps illiterate. Look around: everything is cookie-cuttered. Not only consumer products and goods. Then look in the mirror: the face, eyes, nose—each is just a variation of a form. But that ear, yes, have you studied it hard and long enough? It appears to be an irregular cookie for the nibbling.

More important than a degree, an MFA program grants you a measure of time. As well, it is one of the last sanctioned places in which you can experiment both artistically and socially. You can dress up or dress down, cross genres subtly or audaciously, drink or smoke or not. You can like it with the logic of lights on, or prefer to fumble for figures in the dark. You can even, according to French author Jules Renard, sleep with your husband or wife.

A plethora of MFA programs now exist because a plethora of people do. Since 1936, when the Iowa Writers' Workshop was formally established, the U.S. population has grown officially by

200 million. This accumulation not only of readers and writers but also of all cultural products skews and clutters something fundamental: an MFA program gives an individual a time and place to read and write and make a lifelong friend or two.

The top programs are top because they attract the best students not necessarily because they have the best faculty. Like any classroom setting, an MFA program is only as good as the people who compose it—which is why one applies to the top programs.

Your criteria for applying to an MFA program should be:

- Faculty. Whom do you want to study with? Make sure you like their poems, their aesthetics. You need a mentor, whether or not you'd like one; you can't stand on your own shoulders and the MFA requires someone to chair your thesis.

- Funding: fellowships, assistantships, etc. The point is to take out no loans. Would you like to live with your folks again after grad school? It works for some: cf. Roland Barthes.

- Location. Urban, suburban, rural, overseas? What environment will help you generate the highest quality and quantity of poems? It may not be the most aesthetically pleasing landscape or the hottest, most fashionable city.

Enthusiastic recommendations, an articulate statement of purpose, and an unusual life experience may help, but the writing sample (a selection of your poems) remains the primary criterion for admission. Be aware, however, that all items are important. The statement of purpose, for example, demands that you know your audience: poets and professors who sit on an obligatory committee for which they must read hundreds of statements each year. Reviewing yours for a few minutes, they are looking for a sentence or paragraph that will help them reject your application. There is no reason to be upset; this is understandable, efficient, and human. Write a statement that doesn't give them that (in)excusable sentence.

MFA vs. NYC. On the one hand, there's nothing more sublime than lying down in the middle of Broadway claiming that NYC is your boy/girlfriend and then writing about it later in Brooklyn. On the other, an MFA program arms you with a degree, something to show your parents, and perhaps some teaching experience which will improve your chances for an adjunct gig later on. Pursing one option comes at the opportunity cost of the other, unless you pursue the MFA in NYC. But going that route is something like double-majoring at an Ivy League—everything afterward will seem inferior and you risk being trapped in a state of depression.

While the MFA is considered a terminal degree, the PhD in Creative Writing (or the PhD in English with a Creative

YOU CANNOT MASTURBATE TO THIS SKYLINE EACH MORNING WITHOUT EVENTUALLY BEING PUNISHED

MANHATTAN

Writing dissertation) provides you with even more time to write your first book. Instead of two or three years, now you have four to six. (Without a published or forthcoming book, the PhD, like the MFA, is almost worthless on the job market.) The benefit of doing a PhD, in place of or after completing an MFA, is not to take more writing workshops, but to take more literature courses. Your approach, though, will differ from that of the doctoral students who concentrate on literature or theory. You are not a scholar, and your writing will not look like that of your peers, who are taught to emulate an academic style of writing that is sometimes perspicacious, sometimes unnecessarily opaque. You will instead examine a text—poem, novel, essay—primarily for how it's constructed in order to construct your own texts.

Literary Magazines

As recently as twenty years ago, a young poet might read and submit work to only a few dozen stand-out journals. Today, if you can't find a magazine that you identify with aesthetically or pragmatically, you've not looked hard enough. There are thousands of venues, in print, online, local, national, global—a mess of too many choices, too much to wade through. It all seems incredibly tedious. But think of those nineteenth-century poets and editors who first started literary magazines—wouldn't they find our predicament joyous, ecstatic, and inspiring?

Almost all poets begin the road to book publication by first publishing in magazines. You might consider it a gateway, but it's more helpful to view it as a testing ground for your work. There's no guarantee that any specific number of magazine publications will result in a book, but those publications are small acknowledgments that can keep you going.

Print literary magazines have always been unmemorable but noble miscellanies that take up untold space in editors' offices. Online literary magazines, no less forgettable or miscellaneous, take up only virtual, unseen space.

Literary magazines used to be called little magazines, a label that still seems more accurate, and each has its own highly subjective aesthetic. Most are run on shoestring budgets by an individual or a handful of individuals who are poets and writers themselves. Even if it takes these editors months or an entire year to reject your poems, think no ill-will of them. They are kind, sedulous people.

Perform the thankless work of editing or helping to edit a literary magazine. It is a much different experience from reading a published book or workshopping a peer's poems. The dearth of worthy poems in the slush pile (open submissions) will temporarily boost your confidence about your own work.

Reading hundreds of poems from the slush pile in a single sitting can be alternately serene, frustrating, and once in a while affecting, as if picking through shells on the beach until you find the one or two to carry with you. If possible, read the slush pile alongside other readers or interns in the same room at the same time, sharing the most awful poems and very occasionally a decent or stunning one. Together, that beach combing may begin to feel more energizing, spastic, vital.

Founding an independent press (e.g., City Lights, Alice James Books) or an institution (e.g., Lambda Literary, Before

Columbus Foundation) may seem the most obvious ways to influence what gets put into the canon, but don't overlook the diligence of literary magazines and digital projects. The journal *L=A=N=G=U=A=G=E* (1978–1981) launched Language Poetry, *Callaloo* (1976–) still gives voice to African American poets and writers, and sites like the Electronic Poetry Center (EPC) and UbuWeb (both established in the mid-1990s) hold more "experimental" poetic material than anyone should have to read in a lifetime. And yet one might reasonably go back all the way to *Poetry*, established in 1912 by Harriet Monroe, as an exemplar: the magazine single-handedly ushered in Modernists poets such as Pound, Eliot, Stein, Stevens, Moore, and H.D. And with a $185 million philanthropist's gift in 2003, *Poetry* now stands above the little world of poetry magazines like a benign god: the magazine is the centerpiece of a foundation that sponsors initiatives, fellowships, exhibitions, and educational and outreach programs, and that co-partners with NPR, HBO, PBS, *NYT*, *Reader's Digest*, and just about any other prominent venue.

The truth is that one rarely reads a literary magazine cover to cover. Sometimes one only reads the poem or two that one published in the magazine, which feels perfectly unsatisfying, anti-climatic, and a few weeks or months later humiliating ... the magazine barely touched, just another few quires of paper headed for the recycling bin.

Most scholars don't pay attention to literary journals (which might better be called literary periodicals) because the work is too new and untested. Scholars are concerned with what will endure, which means they are more concerned with the past than with the present. Conceived in the present, literary journals are concerned with the future history they hope to become a part of. This may leave a poet wondering what the point of "make it new" is.

Some think it's easy to stop writing poems if you aren't getting published, but it's quite the opposite. To quit poems can mean quitting oneself. As well, poetic ambition comes and goes—years without the desire to publish a poem, then for no particular reason one sends out a flurry of poems to literary magazines, and then that desire too fades away and it's okay.

Publication

The goal of publication initially feels like it should be to gain a measure of recognition for one's hard work. Which is why that recognition should mention nothing about one's talent.

Talent is quantifiable. Jules Renard: *Talent does not write a single page. It writes 300.* In other words, talent requires hard work and hard work requires time. To be a great poet you have to have a great amount of time. This means making sacrifices of family, friends, love. And there's no knowing who is a great poet until decades or centuries after the poet is dead. Ask yourself again, what could be worth this?

If you write about real events in your life that involve family or friends, don't worry about the truth—literary, emotional, factual—worry about what you can live with once family and friends read the published work … which is often impossible to assess until after the work has been published.

Do you seek publication out of vanity or in order to earn respect or for literary legacy or just because you've put so much time and effort into the poems?

Publishing is a numbers game. You send out as many poems as possible and hope a few stick. The more you send, the better your odds—but the odds are incredibly slim. Develop a taste for rejection. Even after publishing a successful book(s) there will be no end to it. If someday, by chance or success, you begin to receive more acceptances than rejections, you will wonder whether your work is being read at all.

If you take more pleasure in seeing your work or name in print than in sitting down to write the work, you should rethink your work … and then rethink what you want to do with your life.

The more poems you publish, the more each poem will potentially get diluted. The fewer the published poems, the more attention and value they may receive. This isn't the same for prose works. Whereas another John Ashbery collection is more kindling for the wood-burning stove, a new Joyce Carol Oates novel might by itself keep you warm at night.

It's sexiest to be no one. Kind words from a mentor about being a writer no one has heard of; publishers are always looking for the next big somebody to help fund all the nobodies they publish. The sex line may be true of novelists or memoirists, but it's hardly true of poets. Poets are sexiest when they're having or trying to have sex with other poets. It's also when they are trying to be anyone but themselves.

The greater the number of published poems, the greater the opportunity for a critic to find fault with the work. *As compared to her debut collection, these poems are subpar.* Or: *His* Collected Poems *will become an instant classic in no small part because he hanged himself just as described in the book's long series "Meditations of a Hangman."*

If you really want to publish, try posting poems in the "Comments" sections of online pieces that share topics or concerns with your poems. The readership for a well-written essay or article is as receptive, discerning, and interactive as that of any literary journal. In fact, this may be the most efficient way for a poet to establish a credible following, at least until the practice catches on.

Series, Sequence

After one has written and published a number of stand-alone poems—whether lyric or narrative, conventional or experimental—one begins to long for more. One might turn to trying out the short story, or the sustained challenge of a novel. One might, however, begin to put poems together—to make couples of poems, triptychs, or even a longer series or sequence.

The words *series* and *sequence* are often used interchangeably, but in math and science they are discerned: a sequence is a progression of elements (1, 2, 3, 4, 5, etc.), and a series is the summing of the elements of that sequence (1+2+3+4+5, etc.). This might help to understand at least two of the ways poems can come together. Sequence: poems as individual elements that share a common aspect—for example, poems with the same form as in the one-hundred-word each prose poems that make up Joel Brouwer's *Centuries*. Series: poems as individual elements that share a common aspect but also "sum up" over the course of reading them—for example, poems that follow the development of characters as in Rita Dove's *Thomas and Beulah*. An exemplary collection that includes permutations of both series and sequence is Maurice Manning's *Lawrence Booth's Book of Visions*; and Mary Leader's *The Penultimate Suitor* includes "Sequence as Opposed to Series" and "Series as Opposed to Sequence" that pointedly display their differences.

Poems can be grouped after the fact—existing poems retooled to link together in theme, character, place, or structure. Or an overarching idea or concept might come first, say, to write a set of poems that all take place in Alcatraz between two cellmates, or a set that details the lives of zombie superheroes, or a set that all have twenty-seven-word stanzas and are based on twenty-seven photos of pet rabbits. The possibilities are endless and fun to conjure up, but too often a conceptualization feels heavy-handed as one composes. As in any versioning, allow the work to divert and diverge from its initial premise.

Chapbook, Manuscript

Series and sequence often grow into a chapbook: a small collection of poetry (12–36 pages), made by the handful or in print-runs up to 500 copies. Chapbooks often coalesce around a concept, structure, or other means, but they don't have to. The means of production are affordable and easily managed, laid out by hand or software, staple-bound or stitched with needle and thread. Chapbooks abound—and so do chapbook contests. The chapbook is not only a project in itself (some are resplendent, award-winning objets d'art), but also a stepping-stone toward making a full manuscript of poems (48–96 pages).

When you begin putting together a full manuscript, you should understand that no longer is each poem alone: that is, the patterns of any particular poem extend beyond its lines to potentially other poems, other lines. A miscellany of poems gathered together will seem less a miscellany simply by an overarching book title: *Harmonium, U.S. 1, Swarm.*

There is no set way of ordering poems into a manuscript. You figure it out the same way you figure out how to write poems: imitation and variation. After examining dozens of collections, select the one that attracts you the most. Closely read the order of the poems: Why this one first? This one last? Are there patterns between poems, or between the end of one poem and the beginning of the next? Is it really a miscellany? Now reorder the poems yourself. Xerox the book page by page, onto single-sided sheets. (Tearing out all its pages would be fun, but it won't work because the pages are double-sided.) Then, lay them all out on the floor—not the desk—you need a bird's eye view. What do you notice? Are the poems similar in shape, design, form? Are there poems that could be grouped together as sets, based solely on their looks? What are the variations? Any outliers? Begin re-ordering with what you think the first poem should be, then the last. Fill in the others, paying attention to juxtaposition from poem to poem as well as from page to page. Do this over an hour or two, no longer; first impressions are key. Make your own Table of Contents for the new book. Finally, try switching the first and last poems. How much does that single change affect the collection as a whole? Do this de-ordering/re-ordering with other collections, both admirable and loathsome to you.

The majority of readers won't read your collection from beginning to end, one poem after another, but instead will open the book glancingly somewhere in the middle. So consider what you'd like to be your "centerfold" poems just as much as what should be your first and last poems. How naked or exposed can you be in the middle of your book?

Readers don't approach the last poem in a collection in exactly the same way as they do the ends of other types of books—to see how everything turns out. But that last poem—its title and especially the last line—does function as a kind of epitaph for your book. Does the last poem round out the collection or open it up? Does it "answer" questions the book has "proposed" or does it offer new questions, new possibilities?

Collections

Most people read a book—novel, memoir, history, etc.—only once. But a collection of poems on the shelf is different. It's usually slim, doesn't require linear reading, and has greater potential to be pulled down periodically.

On Amazon you will find many poetry collections that have won the National Book Award or Pulitzer with only two or three reviews, whereas you will find everything from coffee filters and nose hair trimmers to cat litter boxes and underpants being reviewing in the thousands. Make no mistake, a book of poems serves comparatively little utility in day-to-day living.

On publication, a 634-page *Collected Poems* garners an 871-word review in the *New York Times*. The review functions as an extended blurb to the book. The grainy grayscale photo of Saturn on the cover covers fifty years of work. There it is now—the new hardback on the floor, next to the matt, because the woman who's written it has misplaced her yoga block.

Our mail-order catalogues of household goods, children's toys, and clothing are brighter, slicker, and eminently more beautiful than our collections of poems. This doesn't have to be. The physical object of a poetry collection could be of such superior materials and design (along the lines of a limited edition artist's book) that it is sought after and prized equally for its material attributes as for its literary value. The price of such collections could be disproportionately expensive vis-à-vis how much they cost to make—$500 or $1,000 per copy—so as to encourage the affluent to make investments and the poor to sell underground copies or make their own imitations.

The best movies are those in which characters are played by unknown actors and actresses; there's no confusion of Character X with Actress Y: Character X exists only as Character X. The best poetry collections function similarly—when you have no idea who is behind the voice(s) in the book. You, and the poet, are free of any shadow knowledge.

Author bios on book jackets seem to cause a great deal of speculation. *Sylvester Kirschbaum splits his time between Provincetown and Provence. Lydia Jongesla divides her time between Barbados and Berlin.* What's the implication here? That the poet has two families or two lovers (one for warm seasons, one for cold); that the poet is an itinerant bohemian who crashes on the couches of other poet-friends; that the poet is rich and deserves the NEA grant in the next line of the bio; or, that since the poet regularly travels across great stretches of land, sea, and air, he or she has important things to say in his or her poems? In a more perfect world, there would be no author bios on book jackets. As is, let us be brief. *Mr. Thoreau has traveled a good deal in Concord*. Or curiously brief. *Anne Carson lives in Canada*.

A blurb is less a genuine recommendation than it is a genuine dare: *Open this book and prove me wrong*.

Book Reviews

The best thing that a review of a poetry collection can do is cite a number of lines or stanzas from the collection itself. This saves the reader from having to hunt down poems from the collection that may have been published online or to find a bookstore or library that has the book, and then skimming its pages herself.

Some poetry reviewers evaluate a collection with questions like: *Are these poems sufficiently new?* and *Does this work further literature?* Other reviewers use a different question:

Could I have written this? And those remaining don't really ask questions; the language of their reviews is mere scaffolding to showcase lines or stanzas excerpted from the book under review.

A negative book review may be doing readers a favor by steering them clear of bad poems, but such a review is as exasperating to read as the book it reviews.

The best thing a negative book review can do is to compare the bad book of poems to a book of poems that succeeds in the aims that the bad book of poems set out for itself.

There's always going to be something wrong with a book review of your own collection. If the review is negative, the wrongness is obvious. If the review is positive, you'll find *something* wrong with it—that it's missed a particular nuanced premise of the work. Failing that, there will forever be an underlying, troublesome detail: a glowing review of a poetry collection yields no glowing sales—so un-glowing that your publisher wonders why she's still publishing your poems.

If we believe in "the death of the author," should we also believe in "the death of the book reviewer"—that is, should we encourage anonymous book reviewing?

A good review should have an effect similar to the report of a pistol that brings a crowd into a lonely room, and having inspected said pistol, shall be determined to have never gone off. Why? Even the best book reviews have the life expectancy of a cloud.

While writing a book review may be a thankless task, editing a literary magazine is a thankless task by an order of magnitude— to have to review book reviewers' work, for example.

Writing Conferences

Writing conferences can provide a certain kind of empathy for a young poet. They can help you make a friend—a real friend, in the flesh—who likes to read and write poems as much as you do.

For well-seasoned poets, a conference offers an opportunity to meet up with poet-friends and acquaintances who are scattered across the country or live abroad. Panels and readings are the ostensible draw, but some of the best events occur in hallways, at bars and restaurants, on public transport, and in taxis and airports where poets exchange ideas and poetic strategies, discuss the state(s) of poetry and the tribulations of publishing, and meet others whose work one has admired from a distance.

But if one doesn't enjoy a certain measure of drinking, gossiping, and carousing, a conference can be dispiriting, even isolating, and make one wonder if it might have been better to stay at home reading and writing poems.

One reason to attend a writing conference is to be disappointed. Attending a panel or reading, your thoughts may become agitated: *That's not accurate, that's not how you do it, that's just bullshit.* Imagined attacks, yes, but real hurt feelings that foment to the point where you want to show up your peers, vowing that while they're at the next panel, you'll be upstairs in your hotel room ferociously writing poems.

The Bread Loaf Writers' Conference, which takes place every summer in the Green Mountains of Ripton, Vermont, is our country's most prestigious. Ninety years running, Bread Loaf continues to be a refuge for poets from the manic, money-driven, nonliterary America ... not necessarily a refuge, that is, for fiction and nonfiction writers who, vying for private meetings with NYC editors and agents, harbor hopes of getting a book deal. Poets don't get book deals; they get headaches after getting too drunk after the reading the night before. The most prestigious spots at the most prestigious conference are the twenty-five "waiterships" awarded each year to promising, unpublished poets and writers who come from myriad backgrounds. Some have families, some are single-parents, some are teachers, some are post-MFAs, some live with their parents—all have made sacrifices for reading and writing, so that they can sit on a small mountain for ten days in August and commiserate over whether their sacrifices are, and will continue to be, worth it.

Bread Loaf Waiters, 2001: Where's Waldo?

Culture Jamming

Poets don't need to feel more guilt than they already do, but if you'd like to "make something happen" beyond the page or the classroom, there is "culture jamming." This is not art with social or political content (as in a protest poem), but real-life action that attempts to transform or upset social or political functioning. For example, in 2004, on the twentieth anniversary of the Bhopal toxic gas disaster, a member of the Yes Men impersonated a Dow Chemical official on BBC News, announcing that Dow was providing $12 billion in compensation to the victims. Days later when it was revealed to be a hoax, the Yes Men were chastised for giving false hope to thousands. But the Yes Men defended their act by arguing that for twenty years the survivors had been hoping for compensation, mostly for medical expenses, from a company that has the ability to improve lives but won't.

Culture jammers don't use poems, per se, but they do employ exacting combinations of word and image in their subversion. Jammers like Adbusters, Guerrilla Girls, Generic Art Solutions, Banksy, and Barbara Kruger try to get us to see social and political issues from slant angles—like the best poems—to get us to re-see what we think we know or what we take for granted. The danger is that once the action gets labeled "art" or "performance art," the work surrenders nearly all of its political efficacy, if not its charm.

Most poets refuse to submit to any authority but their own. Their greatest political act is simply noncompliance. Feeling little control over what surrounds them, they try to dominate the blank page or screen. Their greatest political role: best-possible loser.

Despite those who say that poetry makes nothing happen, humanity continues to be built on a long-standing simile: *Love thy neighbor as thyself.*

Poetic Practices

If you are bored by your poems, others will be, too. There is nothing worse than a poem that inculcates neither adoration nor envy or fury. Your poem needs to move a reader—toward hatred or love. Indifference kills an audience.

The mood of writing will swing from frustration to elation— from thinking that you are a charlatan to believing you are a genius. The other 80–90 percent of the time writing will simply be work, tedium, frustration. Occasionally, though sometimes so infrequently that you question the whole enterprise, you will have a bright moment, analogous to "being in the zone" for an athlete, or you will have a light-headed, timeless moment à la *le petit mort*. The trick is to inhabit such a moment as deeply as possible without being overly self-conscious about the moment, and later to be able to recall the moment so that during all the other moments you long for it.

Read anything you want—fantasy, romance, science fiction, the classics—but read with the eyes of a writer: not only for what the text communicates (content), but for how the text is put together (structure) and, more importantly, how else it might have been put together to different, other effect.

Write something that you don't fully understand as if you understand it perfectly.

Bring your attention to what you are doing. If you are reading a book, read a book. If you are cooking, cook. If you are feeling low, get down on the ground and sleep it off. And if you are lying over your mother's grave and fire ants begin to bite, let your exhalations feed the flame.

Coffee and alcohol? Yes, they are a form of call and response. And cocktails? They are and are not solutions.

Stop now and do absolutely nothing. In a room alone. No reaching for phone or screen or book. Waste your life for the rest of the day, and then another day and another, and see what life is there that you've been ignoring.

Practice diagramming sentences. Correcting everyone else's syntax and grammar will give you something to do on your deathbed.

Ready yourself for writing by trying to draw a perfect circle by hand. In principle it seems easy enough; in practice it's enough to drive you a bit mad—a fine state of mind to begin writing.

Blindfold yourself for an entire weekend just to see what you might break. Routine, bone, silence.

If you enjoy classical myths and tales and want to include them in your poems, inhabit the viewpoints of minor, incidental, or otherwise unheard from characters. These will likely include underappreciated voices of the big three: Race, Class, Gender. Strive to write not out of a generalized empathy but an informed appreciation—because another's thriving can also mean your own.

A great pleasure of writing is writing what people say you shouldn't write.

Don't worry about being part of a poetic "movement." The Metaphysical Poets were given their label by a disapproving critic. The Romantics Poets weren't called the Romantics Poets until almost all of them were dead. And the New York School of Poets were only called that because no one could figure out what to do with them. Don't worry, in other words, about being called names or being a member of a members-only club.

Do not ask a friend if she likes your poem. A negative reply will disappoint you, but so will a positive one. Do not write poems to be liked. Do not be admired for your poems, nor for your actions. Do not be admired at all. Admiration gives you an inflated version of yourself, one that will sooner or later impede the work of writing.

Instead of writing a poem for a certain person or audience, try writing a poem that you don't want anyone to ever read.

Enter a poetry contest not to win, but to have a deadline.

There will come a time when other poets, including close friends, gain critical or commercial success for their work. If you feel envy and perhaps even some rage, that's okay. Conventional wisdom says that in fifty years we'll all be forgotten. You should consider, however, whether you want to live long enough to be forgotten.

It takes a large ego to write in the first place and to keep writing. But over time, the ego must shrink, humility must steadily grow in its stead, and one's sense of self must diminish. It may help at some point to refer to the present tense as the "peasant" tense, or to understand that ordinary tears lubricate your eyeballs every waking minute, about ten ounces per day unless it's been a particularly humiliating day. Figure out how long it takes to get yourself to cry. Use a stopwatch. Would it take longer or shorter if the process didn't have to go through your self-esteem first?

Enjoy yourself being unhappy.

Young children are poet-like not because they are child-like,
per se, but because the patterns of language and culture are not

yet ensconced in their minds. They are unfamiliar objects unto themselves. Having a child will make you a better poet who has less time to write poems.

Be known for the poems you've written, not for the one who wrote the poems.

If you truly want to write poems, make time for writing poems: two to four hour blocks every day. Until you are practiced, it will take the first two hours just to quiet your mind, to find a small open space. If after six months you are not yet obsessed with writing, there's no reason to keep going.

When you are considering a major life decision (job, lover, suicide), the most important question to ask yourself is: *How will this affect my ability to continue writing poems?*

Henry James and Virginia Woolf are not considered poets and yet many poets congregate around their work because their sentences are most wonderful to fall asleep to. Lazily reading a couple of pages of *The Golden Bowl* or *The Waves* in bed works much better than a sleeping pill.

Sleep is as good a muse as anything else.

No other English offering will serve you better as poet than a Bible as Literature course. Not because the Bible heralds religious and historical import, but because it is our greatest post-modern, experimental classic. No text rivals the Bible for its construction from multiple languages, its various and anonymous authors and editors, and its range of genre-bending texts of myth, poetry, history, biography, prophecy, genealogy, surrealism, eroticism, and on and on.

On meeting someone for the first time refrain from asking, *Where are you from?* Instead ask, *Where do you think you are going?* And if you get trapped into a literary corner at a cocktail party, make sure you swing at the biggest thug first. You want to be taken seriously.

Money matters. Take a job that seems like it won't interfere too much with writing. Never take a job that you really enjoy. Soon, you will detest that splendid job and will most assuredly find something splendidly honest yet disastrous to do, like fall in love with someone's spouse despite the fact that it's not generating good poems. Also, remember that a sugar mommy/daddy is an option here as long as she/he is not your real mommy/daddy.

If you wake up one day at age 65 or 75 and feel badly because you have not written a novel or a memoir, don't worry. There will still be time to write a few poems.

There is no end-all-be-all in poetry. The finances certainly aren't there, and fame is an illusion—but so too is pedestrian living. You cannot escape repetition and pain. But practicing bad instead of good habits promises a downward spiral. Artists are masochists unless they are sadists. You can get used to anything: the ecstatic and the atrocious. The taste of chocolate, mind-blowing sex—both reduced to a missing limb, a baby who has choked to death on a grape. To write a poem means not getting used to anything.

Procrastination

It is partly true that a writer washes the kitchen floor or scrubs the bathtub in order to procrastinate writing. Aching over the mop at midnight or tooth-brushing the grout an hour later is also about being physical, about wanting to beat something down, erase something, or to break a sweat. (Writing is as physically rigorous as sunbathing.) But mopping or scrubbing are only second-best to hand-washing an extra-large load of laundry: there's nothing as fulfilling as wringing the neck of a pair of wet jeans or rubbing dog shit out of a pair of grass-stained socks in pre-dawn hours in order to keep mental neurosis at bay.

Reading a guide to writing poems is a perfectly satisfactory way to procrastinate writing poems.

Amateur poets expect their lines to descend from on high or to be whispered in their ear by a muse. Nothing could be further from what happens in practice. For writing is all practice. Talent is what posers enjoy talking about on game shows and blind dates.

Be calm for a moment. Observe closely how your breath goes in and out without your having to do anything. Feel it there at the back of your sinuses and throat. It keeps moving slowly in and out. Is that how you want your poems to come to you, without your having to do any work?

Inspiration comes after writing, not before.

Don't mistake the silence of the page for the silence of God. It's merely eternity sticking out its hand, slapping you around a little. If the blank white page intimidates or frightens you, simply try closing your eyes and staring at the blank black screen that has always been there.

If you think doing research is procrastinating the writing of a poem, make the poem itself the research. The special collections sections of university libraries are a good starting point: they harbor little known texts, ephemera, and other gems that can't be digitized.

As soon as writing gets easy, you know something is terribly wrong.

Everything should be an opportunity for a poem. A visit to a museum, a trip to the grocery store, a fall down a flight of stairs. Painting, produce, squash.

An hour of procrastination can ruin a day of writing. The minute you stop writing begins the hour you could have finished the poem.

Like French Troubadours between the twelfth and fourteenth centuries, when you feel down about your work, prod yourself with a dirty little mantra. It doesn't have to be ornate; a run-of-the-mill *fuck me fuck me fuck me* suffices. Though something with a bit more spruce like *my anus aches appreciably* helps to purge the mind, literally, so that you won't fill your poems with vulgarity.

There is no such thing as "writer's block." There is indolence, insomnia, and finally death.

End Notes

The measure of a successful life with poetry may be that one has yet to end it on purpose.

Why don't more poets kill themselves? Because it's not worth it if you can't write about it afterward. And why don't more poets who kill themselves leave a note? Because writing a suicide note is counterproductive.

Dear Friends: if you plan on dying by your own hand, don't use pills. Swallowing is simply another way of marking time.

As seen in a number of cases, a poet's self-murder can lead to fame. But it is hard to find even the most righteous of critics who will advocate the practice. And with good reason: How many straight-up critics have ever become famous after killing themselves?

Those who pronounce the death, near-death, or suicide of poetry are the same people who are keeping it alive.

Poems are not made to mesmerize us as screens do, or to prevent bullets from shattering bones, or to cement enemies' hands together in celebration of the world's diversity. Poems only do what they do. Ask too much of them and you risk dying many times before actually having to do the deed.

Practically speaking, poems never die; they merely go unread for so long that people forget they were ever made. For they are always made, carefully constructed as houses of cards on desks in actual houses or haphazardly, but lovingly, constituted as remnants in metaphorical ashtrays.

Old poets may claim that in all the cosmos nothing is as alive as our dead. We know it's true even if we tell the dying that they're simply returning to what was never once alive. Poetry, too, is a form of death, as it only exists when we live with it. And the poems that we never read or write aren't any more dead than the lives we never live.

If you live long enough, you will come to understand that the things that have brought you meaning—parents, friends, work, play, reading, writing, publications—are also the things that will leave you meaningless. One by one, you'll have to let them go. If you're lucky.

You begin an elegy because you want someone else to feel as wounded as you do. As you keep writing, the writing prolongs the grief and that someone else turns out to be you.

After your parents die, you understand what language really is, where it leads to—divesting us of drama and content, reducing us to basic forms. You do not want to but you have to accept, in the end, that Mother and Father are merely trochees.

A poet may try to conquer death by writing, but it's ridiculous. She can't even conquer sleep. Or she waits all day long for sleep—for the chance to see the dead on the other side of it, in a dream.

A eulogy is a form meant to honor the dead but is written for the living. It would be better, however, to write and give a eulogy to the dying before they go. For reflection, lament, and memorial, survivors already have the form of the elegy. And one form is more than enough.

There is no meter for grief.

Building a monument or having a gravestone made is not to remind you of the past event or deceased relative, but to help you forget them. If there is something physical to represent them, then you don't have to do that work yourself. This is why scattering a beloved's ashes, say, over the ocean is a terrible idea. You can't have the entire Pacific do the work of grief.

The end of mourning is a page intentionally left blank.

Neither love nor death joins us forever; only things said to be ineffable do. So when you first wake up in morning and gaze into the ceiling and think *I'm still here*, pick up the book or the keyboard. Do the one thing that would make today as good as any other day to die.

Write.

Epilogue

I am happiest when feeling the first pulses from the showerhead, and saddest when I have to shut off the water and leave. This sadness even beats that of having to depart the warm bed in the thick of winter for the cold kitchen floor because the baby is crying and hungry. Most important are the thoughts I have in the shower. They are free-flowing, though not often wild or fantastical, and at least one of them almost always surprises. My mind seems to best synthesize information when my body is unclothed yet unexposed. And I imagine that I'm not unique in finding the morning shower the high point of the day. After I step out, it's all downhill.

For all the tired clichés about singing in the shower, I have to admit that I'm never more inspired or humbled than when I stand in that solitary space. It's not the being naked. It's the fact of enjoying the hot, clean water for an unprescribed amount of time, or until the water heater is emptied. It's the fact that I am allowed this hot shower once a day—more if I want—and that the vast majority of the people in the world—in fact, the vast majority of all who have ever lived—do not enjoy this seemingly banal event. And if I begin to masturbate in the shower (as occasionally a married man with toddlers may do), then I use more hot, clean water, and after ejaculation I feel as pathetic and solemn as if I were seated in church asking the good Lord for something I don't deserve. Yet, I believe that it's better to kneel in the shower to pray—for inspiration, for humility—than to do it Sunday morning at mass making a pretense out of reverence before others.

*

I sent those two above paragraphs to an editor at *Poets & Writers* magazine, who'd asked me to write a missive on "what inspires me as a poet." In reply I was told, "[T]he physical details of the recommended practice—in this case a long shower—need to take a backseat to more specifics on how the act influences your writing … and please leave the masturbation part out. In this context, the subject isn't going to sit well with the majority of the readers of our magazine." I didn't feel personally slighted by this response as much as I felt some kind of sorry for readers who don't masturbate or won't acknowledge masturbation as a fundamental human act. More importantly, I was disappointed that my point was missed: out of all the possible transcendental places in one's house (e.g., fireplace, bedroom, rooftop), the shower—plain, homely, ephemeral—should take the top spot.

The history of my muse is brief. The word "shower" comes to us from Old English ("light fall of rain, hail, sleet, etc."), and the mad geniuses who first installed in-house waterfalls were the Greeks and the Romans. The former invented indoor plumbing, and the latter bathhouses. When both empires bit the dust, sadly both inventions pretty much did as well. At least until the middle of the nineteenth century, when the French military began using communal showers to clean up prisoners (more efficient than providing individual baths). Soon thereafter, doctors and scientists began to realize that regular washing might help prevent the spread of disease. In the twentieth century, indoor plumbing became a significant marker of modernity—no more pissing in the woods, or freezing while defecating in an outhouse, but also no more poetic running with pail to the well. Post–World War II, shower arms and showerheads began popping up over bathtubs everywhere— or, if space was tight, it was simple to put in a shower stall. Showers and poems proliferated.

One of the initial arguments for the shower was its water-saving potential. An average bath expends about 20 gallons of water while an average shower expends about 12 or 10 or 8 or ... well, fewer ... it all depends on how long your shower lasts and if your showerhead is low-flow. Low-flow showerheads emit between 0.375 and 1.5 gallons per minute, whereas old school showerheads emit between 3 and 8 gallons per minute. Low flow doesn't mean low pressure, by the way. (Number one criterion for apartment hunting: *Honey, did you check the water pressure in the shower?* Number two: *Are there built-in bookshelves for all your damn books?*)

I recall once arguing eco-poetics with a girlfriend who was doing a PhD in Environmental Studies. She'd decided we shouldn't have children because doing so would take up too many natural resources. But when I suggested that maybe she could just cut down on her twice-a-day (morning and post-gym) twenty-minute showers, she adamantly refused. "And if we truly want to conserve," I said, "we should be taking 'navy' showers—turn the water on to get wet, turn it off to lather, and turn it on again to rinse." "More eco-poetics," she said, "what's the fun in that?"

None of us was born a poet. None of us was born shower obsessed. No child wants to take a shower instead of a bath (and many of us didn't want the bath either). At some point, encouraged or demanded by our parents, each of us took that first step over the tub or shower stall sill by ourselves. I was about eight years old when I began showering every morning before school. My process of methodical scrubbing has gone practically unaltered for nearly forty years: I wash from the head downward, in a side-to-side movement, until I reach the feet where the bar of soap rubs between each toe. The only change over the years has been in making double sure that I never touch the genitalia again after washing the feet, for fear of transferring any potential foot fungus to the crotch. And every time I begin to wash, I am super self-conscious of what I am doing; the ritual feels as new and important as it did when, as a child, I was first admonished that the world is a dirty place, and I must get every last one of my surfaces and crannies clean!

The strange thing about showering is that it's both utterly personal and highly universal. (Is the same true of poem-making?) On the one hand, the details of my showering habits have never been shared with anyone until now, and I can imagine that those details—save perhaps my fungal phobia—are very similar to those of millions of others. On the other hand, my wife views the shower as her most-prized personal space, and her showering habits, aside from the products she uses, are completely unknown to me. The shower sex scene may appear idiosyncratically in our collective memories, but showering itself seems to be a routinized secret.

One might argue that I'm overstating the case. It's just a fucking shower. (These are just fucking words.) Aren't they all virtually the same? Showers are supremely low-tech; even Thoreau in his cabin might have fashioned one by pouring a bucket of pond water over his head. And if we're talking about the modern shower stall, it's really just an upright coffin with a hose on one end and a drain on the other. Low-tech, yes, but it's unthinkable that we could do without them today. (Must one have a poem-a-day?)

Beyond the quotidian, I can recount my life by the poesy of the showers in which I have scrubbed myself. The shower of childhood: 1970s sea-green tiles with mint-green grouting. The shower of high school: communal—dirty yellow walls, white hot shower jets—where the goal wasn't to get clean but to get wet enough so that the gym teacher would hand you a lifesaving, genitalia-covering towel that smelled of burnt dryer lint. The shower of college: institutional, sterile, at the end of a carpeted hallway. The shower of graduate school: a patchouli-scented stall which could be transformed into a tantric love cube with the right partner. The shower of middle age: rife with accoutrements such as organic loofas, European shower gels, and an array of shampoos and conditioners—the scent of each one is a Proustian memory trigger. As for the shower of old age, I can only speculate that it'll be emblematic of old age: in a place where I've always been happy and alone, suddenly someone will have to help me while pretending he or she is alone.

Which makes me think of the shower I most miss, which I began missing long before it was gone. For seventeen years my mother-in-law, whom I loved deeply, battled colon cancer. Two years before she died she moved into her "dream home"—a one bedroom midtown Manhattan apartment where she had everything renovated to nearly her every wish. Although the view from that nineteenth floor was lovely, I was more enamored with the thousands of iridescent, mother-of-pearl, three-quarter-inch square tiles that walled the apartment's shower. When my wife, our son, and I visited, the apartment became chaotic and claustrophobic—the sole refuge was the shower. While behind its glass door, I would run a finger over the tiles and imagine the hands of the laborer who had laid and grouted each one, which was odd because I'd never contemplated who, for example, had put down the hardwood floors or hung all the doors or built the custom-made Japanese false wall that separated the living and dining areas.

I would take extra-long showers and try to fathom my mother-in-law's death, as mediated by the shower: *Will this be my final time in this space? Will she live another few months until we can visit again and I can admire this iridescence?* The last shower, in fact, took place three months after she died when the apartment had sold. Without much thought, I gave myself a perfunctory wash and then dashed down and out to the front the building where a U-Haul, loaded with items my wife wanted to take back home to New Orleans, was double-parked. What strikes me now is how those tiles are still with me—not as ceramic sheets that can be bought online, as I've discovered, at Walmart—but as a collective marker of my mother-in-law's own iridescence.

This personal history, however, is of the *place* of the shower, not of the act of showering itself. Aside from the handful of sexcapades, who can conjure up the details of any particular moment in the shower? Analogous to Walter Benjamin's insight about mass-produced artworks, each shower is repeatable, mechanized, and forgettable; to employ his term, no shower has a unique "aura." But this is exactly why I believe all showers are special: none is memorable, but each in the moment of its occurring takes on a workaday reverence. There is no better (or worse) time to inspect one's body, with all its bizarre topographies (ankles, anyone?) and splendid imperfections (asymmetrical testicles, that juxtaposition of anal and vaginal openings, and those childhood scars that reify our individual stories). The body is the object through which knowledge and memory of all other objects of the world has been collected— and it becomes hyper visible, glistening, in the shower. The genuine beauty is that as soon as one reaches for the towel and gets out, one forgets all about the experience—only to do it over again in a day or less.

At once the shower is familiar and strange. When I say "indoor waterfall," for example, you may picture some kind of artificial nature scene in a contained space, like one of those faux backyard rock fountains. Like a waterfall, a shower isn't there exactly to service us. It exists. You turn it on. It runs nonstop. It exists. You turn it off. You *service* the shower.

In other words, the shower is as much there for you as you are there for it. This could sound a bit ludicrous, but when reconsidering my initial premise—that I find inspiration in the shower—the shower begins to take on a meaning I didn't assign it. My missive to *Poets & Writers* was inappropriate not because it was offensive but because it was impractical. If it's three in the afternoon and I'm stuck in a rut of a poem, I don't go hop in the shower and make out with my muse. That's not how muses or showers work.

Fundamentally, the shower is a mystery. It's a room within a room within a room (home, bathroom, shower), and yet it's full of nothing until you arrive. The paradox is that, like a cathedral, it's not a space that you occupy as much as a space that occupies you. To re-inspect the cliché, the interesting feature about singing in the shower may not be that nobody else is around to hear how awful your song sounds. It's that the song you sing in the shower doesn't have to mean anything. Just like a poem.

ACKNOWLEDGMENTS

Thank you to my parents, James Yakich (1935–2013) and Marjorie Yakich (1940–2014), for always supporting my endeavors, no matter how wandering, inscrutable, or poetic. Thank you to Chris Schaberg whose encouragement, collaboration, and very dear friendship propelled this book. Thank you to everyone at Bloomsbury, especially Haaris Naqvi, Mary Al-Sayed, and Balaji Kasirajan. Thank you to the editors of *The Atlantic*, *The Boston Review*, *Colombia Review*, *Cream City Review*, *The Millions*, *Omniverse*, *Poets on Teaching*, and *Propeller Magazine* where selections of this book first appeared.

Thank you to my teachers who initially planted certain poetic seeds in my mind: Mary Leader (line as poetic unit, sublimation, trustworthy typos), Andrei Codrescu (poet as subversive), Dave Smith (New Criticism), Roger Kamenetz (O'Hara, Parra), Ann Lauterbach (fragmentation), Shara McCallum (dramatic voice), James Kimbrell (verdant sound), Eric Naiman (Nabokov), Tom Russell (guilty bystander), Randall Kenan (Baltasar Gracián), and Mark Winegardner ("sexiest to be no one").

Thank you to Loyola University for a Marquette Fellowship that helped me complete this book. Thank you to my students Erin Little and Stewart Sinclair who peer-reviewed excerpts of this book.

Thank you to the numerous poets, writers, and artists with whom I've talked shop.

Thank you to Joel Kelly for his friendship and aeronautics.

Thank you to Ray Buffalo for keeping the fire going.

Thank you to Plater Robinson for his indefatigable example of vulnerability and courage.

Thank you to Dmitri Khorov for teaching me how to be.

Thank you to my sister Stephanie and brother-in-law Nick for their unwavering support and love.

Thank you to my children Owen and Samara for being patient as Daddy worked upstairs on his silly book.

And most importantly, thank you to my wife Annie for whom I have no words, only love.

Credits

All illustrations are the author's with the exception of the following: the rabbit/duck illustration is attributed to psychologist Joseph Jastrow; the young woman/old woman illustration is attributed to psychologist E.G. Boring.

Emily Dickinson's recipe/poem is in the public domain and comes from the Archives and Special Collections of Amherst College.

Touro. Here. For Life. is a registered logo of Touro Infirmary of New Orleans.

INDEX